The 500 Hidden Secrets of

ISTANBUL

INTRODUCTION

The 500 Hidden Secrets of Istanbul is not your typical city guidebook; it is more of an homage to the multifaceted traits that make Istanbul so unique. So you won't come across the usual touristic hotspots or venues that have already been written about exhaustively. Instead, in this book, you will find underappreciated historic architecture exuding the city's long and multicultural past. You'll find restaurants where local chefs are reinterpreting Turkish cuisine, but also modest backstreet restaurants where traditional dishes are served with a loving consistence.

This book will guide you to the bars where Istanbul's younger generation sips on craft cocktails, as well as to all the places they head to later in the evening, to dance or to listen to live music. You'll learn where to go to admire more modern architecture, and you'll discover the places where the most interesting artistic and cultural projects are exhibited and celebrated. You'll be recommended to hop on the ferry and explore Kadıköy (the Asian Side), especially the young and bohemian Moda neighbourhood. And when you need a break from the city's beloved chaos, this book will tell you where to go on the islands.

The 500 Hidden Secrets of Istanbul is a book for inhabitants and visitors, but most of all it's one local's love letter to the city.

HOW TO USE THIS BOOK?

This book lists 500 things you need to know about Istanbul in 100 different categories. Most of these are places to visit, with practical information to help you find your way. Others are bits of information that help you get to know the city and its habitants. The aim of this guide is to inspire, not to cover the city from A to Z.

The places in this guide are listed with their address, in which Mh. stands for 'Mahalle' (neighbourhood in English), Cd. stands for 'Cadde' (Avenue) and Sk. stands for 'Sokak' (Street). Each place is also given a number from 1 to 500, and each address is appointed to a district. These districts and numbers allow you to find the locations on the maps at the beginning of the book: first look for the map of the corresponding district, then look for the right number. A word of caution: these maps are not detailed enough to allow you to find specific locations in the city. You can obtain an excellent map from any tourist office or in most hotels. Or the addresses can be located on a smartphone.

Please also bear in mind that cities change all the time. The chef who hits a high note one day may be uninspiring on the day you happen to visit. The hotel ecstatically reviewed in this book might suddenly go downhill under a new manager. Or the cafe recommended as one of the '5 cafes where the locals hang out' might be empty on the night you visit. This is obviously a highly personal selection. You might not always agree with it. If you want to leave a comment, recommend a bar or reveal your favourite secret place, please visit the website *www.the500hiddensecrets.com* or follow *@500hiddensecrets* on Instagram or Facebook and leave a comment.

THE AUTHOR

Feride Yalav fell in love with Istanbul in 2011 whilst sitting beneath the Galata Bridge and watching the old ferries glide across the Golden Horn. Ever since then she has been exploring Istanbul and writing about her discoveries for local and international publications.

From neighbourhood profiles to in-depth interviews with eccentric personalities to reflections on the city's effervescent culture, cuisine and history, Istanbul has been a source of seemingly endless inspiration for Feride. It has also been an enigma that continually divulges something new, because Istanbul is a place where opposites somehow create a delicate balance. Istanbul is ancient and it is young, it is confounding and irritating but also breathtakingly beautiful. And even in the moments when she's exhausted from its crowds and its noise, Istanbul always presents Feride with another beguiling morsel that allows her to continue exploring and sharing.

With this book, Feride hopes that you will also fall in love with Istanbul, a city that is inherently unfathomable and often maddening, but always profoundly inspiring.

Feride would like to thank *"Elif Savari Kızıl, my close friend and the photographer of this book – your images have always been the perfect companions to my words; the Luster team and especially my editor Dettie Luyten – it was wonderful working with you; and my husband Peter Heckeroth – thank you for always being by my side."*

ISTANBUL

overview

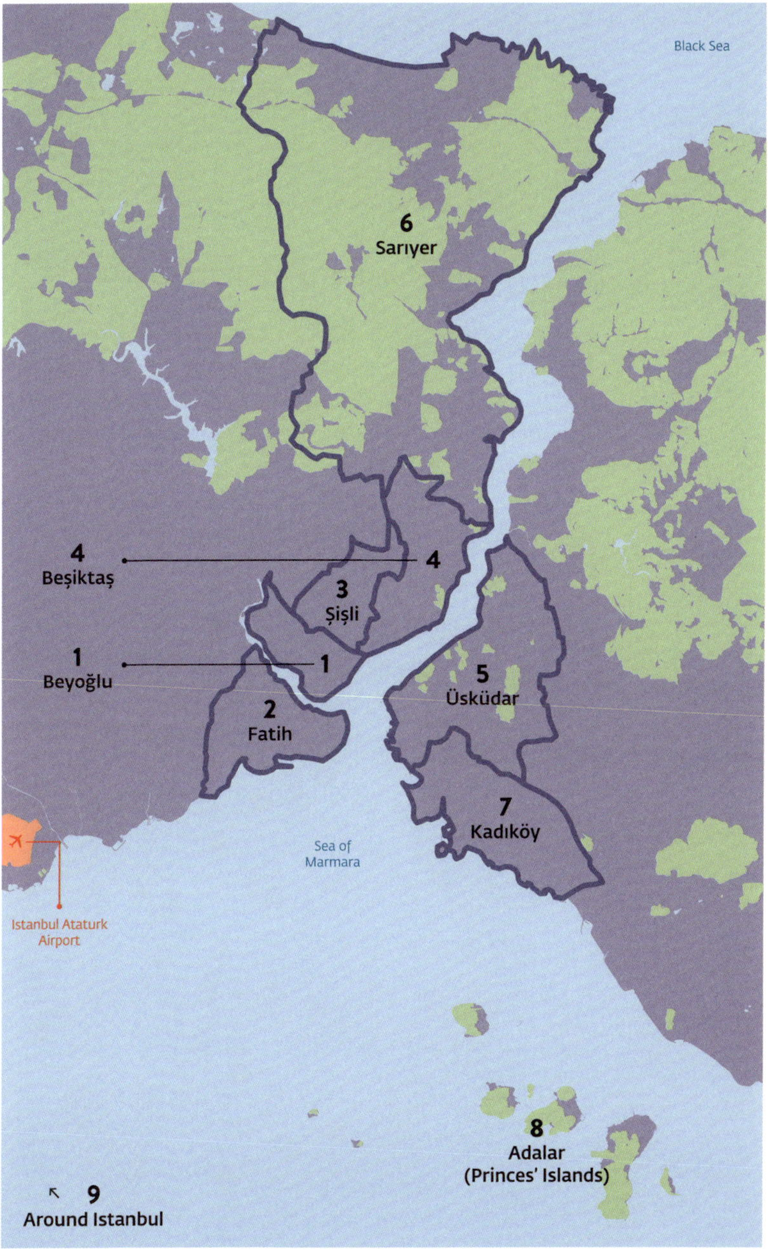
Black Sea
6
Sarıyer
4
Beşiktaş
4
3
Şişli
1
Beyoğlu
1
2
Fatih
5
Üsküdar
7
Kadıköy
Sea of
Marmara
Istanbul Ataturk
Airport
8
Adalar
(Princes' Islands)
9
Around Istanbul

Map 1
BEYOĞLU

EAT – DRINK – SHOP – BUILDINGS – DISCOVER – CULTURE – SLEEP – WEEKEND – RANDOM

EAT – DRINK – SHOP – BUILDINGS – DISCOVER – CULTURE – SLEEP – WEEKEND – RANDOM

Map 2

FATIH

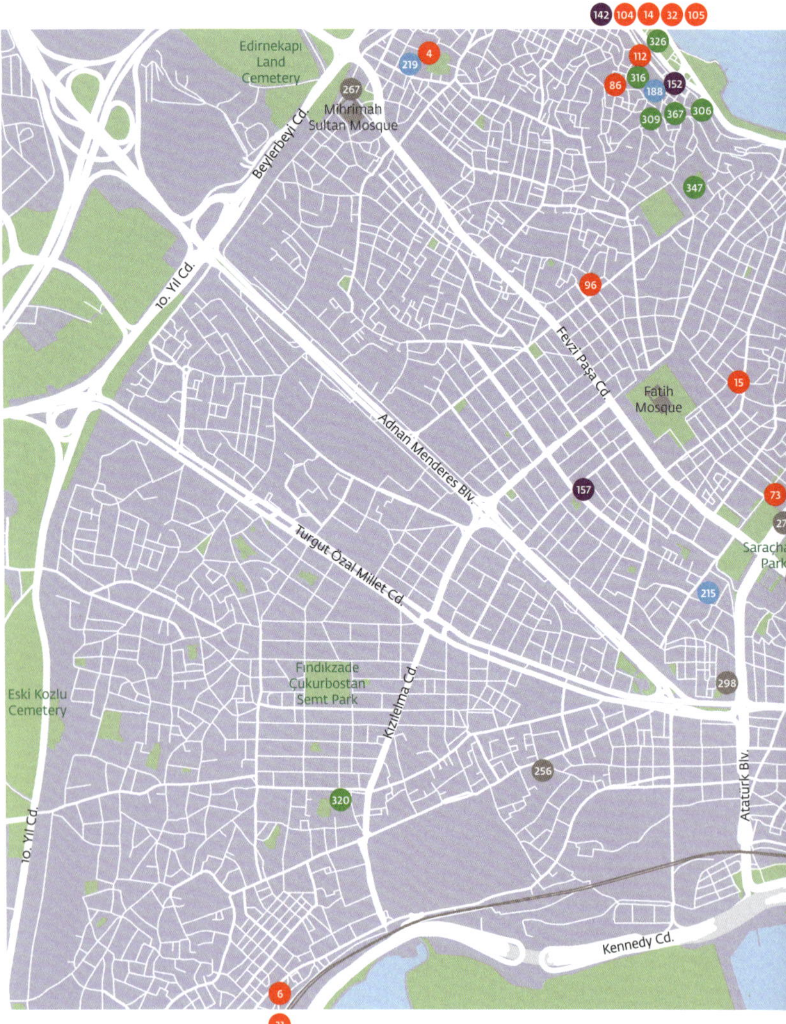

EAT – DRINK – SHOP – BUILDINGS – DISCOVER – CULTURE – SLEEP – WEEKEND – RANDOM

EAT – DRINK – SHOP – BUILDINGS – DISCOVER – CULTURE – SLEEP – WEEKEND – RANDOM

Map 3

ŞIŞLI *and* (SOUTH) BEŞIKTAŞ

EAT – DRINK – SHOP – BUILDINGS – DISCOVER – CULTURE – SLEEP – WEEKEND – RANDOM

EAT – DRINK – SHOP – BUILDINGS – DISCOVER – CULTURE – SLEEP – WEEKEND – RANDOM

Map 4
(NORTH) BEŞIKTAŞ *and* (NORTH) ÜSKÜDAR

EAT – DRINK – SHOP – BUILDINGS – DISCOVER – CULTURE – SLEEP – WEEKEND – RANDOM

Map 5

(SOUTH) ÜSKÜDAR

EAT – DRINK – SHOP – BUILDINGS – DISCOVER – CULTURE – SLEEP – WEEKEND – RANDOM

Map 6

SARIYER

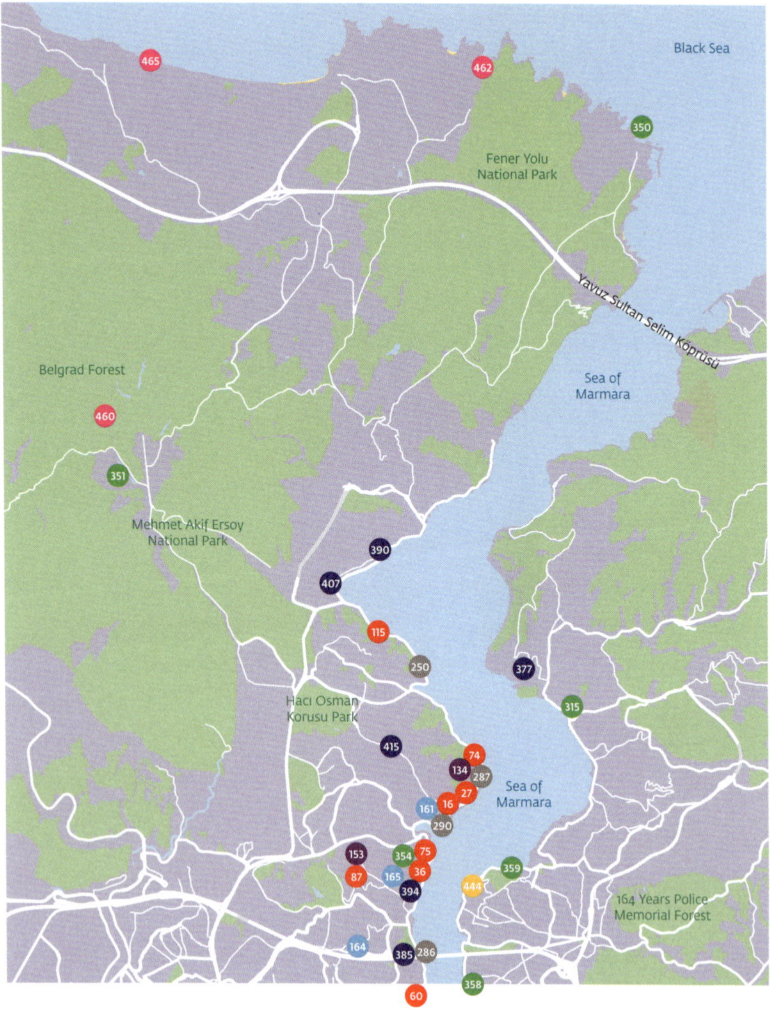

EAT – DRINK – SHOP – BUILDINGS – DISCOVER – CULTURE – SLEEP – WEEKEND – RANDOM

Map 7
KADIKÖY

EAT – DRINK – SHOP – BUILDINGS – DISCOVER – CULTURE – SLEEP – WEEKEND – RANDOM

Map 8
ADALAR (PRINCES' ISLANDS)

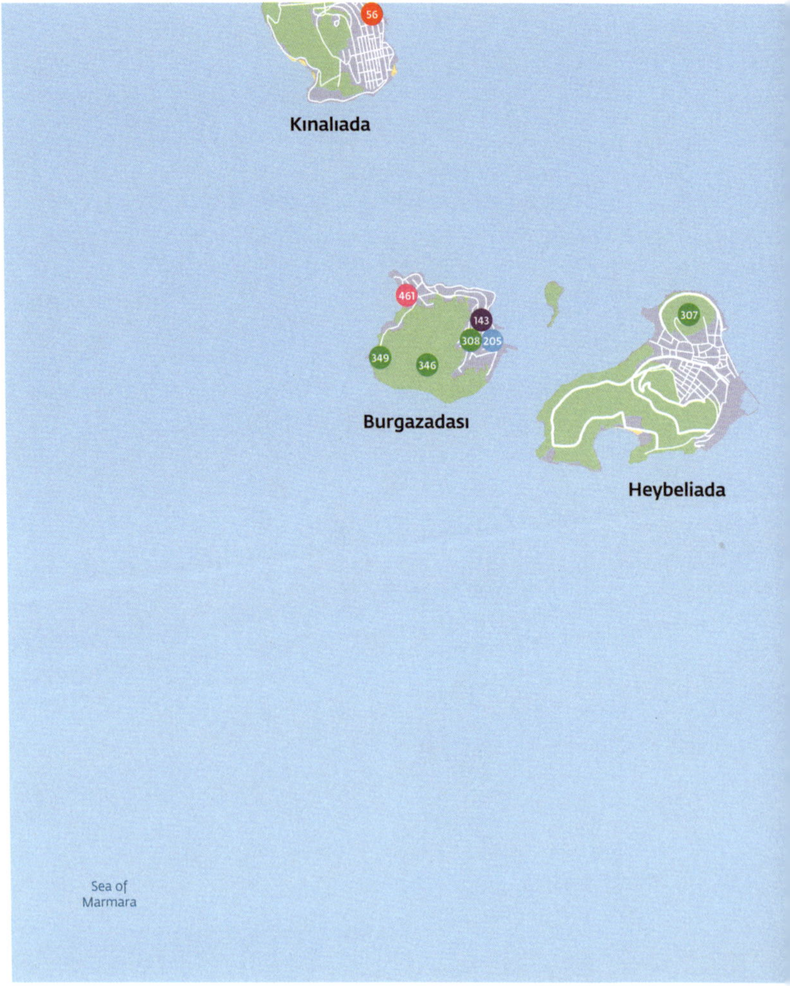

421
285
281
283
282
Dil Burnu Tabiat Park
284
318
29
463
Büyükada National Park
310
Sedef Adası
Büyükada

Map 9

AROUND ISTANBUL

EAT – DRINK – SHOP – BUILDINGS – DISCOVER – CULTURE – SLEEP – WEEKEND – RANDOM

Black Sea
450
451
Şile
464
447
Polonezköy
Nature Park
448
Sabiha Gökçen
Airport

BALAT SAHIL RESTORAN

115 PLACES TO EAT OR BUY GOOD FOOD

5 places for

CLASSIC TURKISH CUISINE

1 **HÜNKAR**
Harbiye Mh.
Mim Kemal Öke Cd. 21
Şişli ③
+90 212 225 46 65
hunkarlokantasi.com

An upscale *esnaf* (tradesmen) restaurant with daily made dishes that reflect the kind of food you'd find in homes all over Turkey. Consistency in excellence has made Hünkar an establishment where regulars take comfort in dishes such as slow cooked lamb wrapped in eggplant or *kadınbudu köfte* (meatballs fried in egg batter).

2 **BORSA**
Harbiye Mh.
Gümüş Cd. 4
Şişli ③
+90 212 232 42 01
borsarestaurants.com

Another upscale establishment that prides itself on consistency, Borsa presents a menu of almost every classic Turkish dish imaginable and serves it true to its original recipe and ingredients. From artichoke confit in olive oil to black cabbage stuffed with lamb, Borsa offers the perfect introduction to the Turkish kitchen.

3 **HACI ABDULLAH**
Hüseyinağa Mh.
Atıf Yılmaz Cd. 9-A
Beyoğlu ①
+90 212 293 85 61
haciabdullah.com.tr

Skip the touristic İstiklal Caddesi restaurants and head to one of Taksim's most established eateries serving homecooked-style Turkish food. Underneath a dome of colourful glass and past a row of decorative pickle jars, you can choose from the daily made specials in a cafeteria-style display.

4 ASITANE

Dervişali Mh.
Kariye Cami Sk. 6
Fatih ②
+90 212 635 79 97
asitane.business.site

In the garden of a restored Ottoman mansion, guests of Asitane travel back in time with the exceptional dishes of Ottoman Palace cuisine. Through the study of historic documents, the Asitane team has been presenting such unique tastes as cinnamon and clove flavoured chicken stew or almond soup with pomegranate seeds.

5 MAHIR LOKANTASI

Cumhuriyet Mh.
Tavukçu Fethi Sk. 28-B
Şişli ③
+90 212 234 93 94
mahirlokantasi.com

You'd never notice this restaurant hidden away on the second floor of an apartment building overlooking the busy avenue near the Osmanbey metro. An exceptionally friendly staff, fresh homecooked-style regional dishes from all over Turkey and a highly recommended *lahmacun* (made to order) await in this cosy neighbourhood restaurant.

5 MAHIR LOKANTASI

5 *of the best*
KEBAB JOINTS

6 **ALI HAYDAR**
Kocamustafapaşa Mh.
Gümüşyüzük Sk. 6
Fatih ②
+90 212 584 21 62

Ali Haydar is famous for two things: being the subject of a famous TV show from the 1990s and absolutely amazing kebab. Every night Ali Usta himself sits at the copper hooded grill turning several rows of kebabs and whole eggplants until they're just right, while patrons raise their glasses of *rakı* and sing along to the street musicians.

7 **KEBAPÇI ENVER USTA'NIN YERI**
Şahkulu Mh.
İlk Belediye Cd. 19-A
Beyoğlu ①
+90 212 252 29 41

Hailing from Gaziantep, one of Turkey's kebab capitals, Enver Usta knows exactly how to create carnivore magic with his grill. This favourite local lunch spot is a no-fuss and cash-only restaurant where the perfectly chargrilled *kemikli tavuk* (chicken wings) come highly recommended.

8 **ULUDAĞ KEBABÇISI**
Şenlikköy Mh.
Sahil Yolu
İstanbul Cd. 12
Florya ⑨
+90 212 624 95 90
uludagkebap.com

Overlooking a beautiful sandy beach and the seemingly endless sea, Uludağ Kebabçısı is the place to try *iskender:* a dish composed of sliced *pide* bread topped with thin slices of döner meat and covered in tomato sauce. Make sure to wait for the extra helping of melted butter before you dig in.

9 **ADANA OCAKBAŞI**
Bozkurt Mh.
Bay Sungur Sk. 2
Şişli ③
+90 212 247 01 43
adanaocakbasi.com

Established in 1978, Adana Ocakbaşı is hidden away on a side street past the clamorous main avenue of Ergenekon. Another no-frills hang-out where the kebab is the main event, you'll find locals sitting around, drinking *rakı* and enjoying fresh grilled meat varieties that were, moments ago, being prepared on the grill right in front of them.

10 **ZÜBEYIR OCAKBAŞI**
Şehit Muhtar Mh.
Bekar Sk. 28
Beyoğlu ①
+90 212 293 39 51
zubeyirocakbasi.com.tr

You'll have to reserve in advance to get a table at this very popular kebab restaurant on two floors in a historic building off bustling İstiklal. After taking your pick from the tray of meze (cold appetizers), which will be brought to you, order a mixed plate of kebab freshly made at the copper hooded hearth.

The 5 best

NEIGHBOURHOOD MARKETS

11 **TARIHI KASTAMONU / INEBOLU MARKET**
Küçük Piyale Mh.
Toprak Tabya Sk. 28-30
Beyoğlu ①

According to rumours, this is the market where Istanbul's top chefs pick up their gourmet products early in the morning on Sundays. Locals also come here for their farm fresh eggs, produce and cheese varieties. Deeply reliant on the seasons, you'll find the most variety in the summer when everything in nature is in bloom.

12 **BEŞIKTAŞ MARKET**
Türkali Mh.
Nüzhetiye Cd. 66
Beşiktaş ③

This huge Saturday *pazarı* (market) is the place to mingle with the locals who arrive with their shopping trolleys in tow, picking out the best among the landscape of colourful produce. Upstairs you'll also find more stalls selling clothing, accessories and home goods at cheap prices.

13 **FERIKÖY ORGANIC MARKET**
Cumhuriyet Mh.
Gökkuşağı Sk.
Şişli ③

This Saturday market is held in a parking lot amongst Bomonti's high-rise apartments and is strictly organic. You'll find produce, bread, cheese, legumes and much more. Locals like to have their breakfast at one of the stands making fresh *gözleme* (thin griddled dough with filling).

14 BALAT MARKET

Balat Mh.
Mahkeme Altı Cd.
Fatih ②

Every Sunday this small market sets up its stands early in the morning among the historic surfaces of the Balat neighbourhood. You'll only find locals here who pick up their fresh produce, cheese, strained yoghurt, butter, honey, dried fruits and more. Make sure to buy some Taşköprü garlic, the market's food celebrity.

15 FATIH MARKET

Zeyrek Mh.
Nevşehirli İbrahim Paşa Cd.
Fatih ②

One of Istanbul's largest markets (only on *Çarşamba* / Wednesdays) is also in one of its most conservative neighbourhoods, so make sure to dress modestly. You'll find yourself in a maze of stalls overflowing with a colour spectrum of fresh fruits and vegetables, as well as clothing, accessories and home goods.

11 TARIHI KASTAMONU / INEBOLU MARKET

5 excellent

MODERN TURKISH RESTAURANTS

16 **ARAKA**
Yeniköy Mh.
Kapalı Bakkal Sk. 8
Sarıyer ⑥
+90 212 223 72 23

Former chef of the famously innovative (but sadly defunct) Müzedechanga restaurant, Pınar Taşdemir has returned with her own personal culinary project. In a minimal space of exposed brick, wood and earthenware, the talented female chef's creative whims are led by seasonality to create masterfully unique dishes.

17 BASTA! STREET FOOD BAR

17 **BASTA! STREET FOOD BAR**
Caferağa Mh.
Sakız Sk. 1-A
Kadıköy ⑦
+90 216 414 08 65
bastafood.com

What happens when two former haute cuisine chefs decide to open a street food bar? The classic Turkish street food *dürüm* (wrap) is filled with gourmet ingredients such as slow cooked lamb or bonito, for example. Let's not forget the burger with a juicy lamb patty and eggplant mayonnaise between homemade brioche buns.

18 **YENI LOKANTA**
Tomtom Mh.
Kumbaracı Ykş. 66
Beyoğlu ①
+90 212 292 25 50
yenilokanta.com

When renowned chef Civan Er opened up his own restaurant in 2013 it became an instant favourite in the 'New Anatolian Kitchen' movement. Inside a modern space with hand-painted tiles and green pendant lights, the seasonally changing menu reflects the traditional tastes and ingredients from every corner of Turkey with a creative twist.

19 **NEOLOKAL**
AT: SALT GALATA BUILDING
Arap Cami Mh.
Bankalar Cd. 11
Beyoğlu ①
+90 212 244 00 16
neolokal.com

Another important chef in the 'New Anatolian Kitchen' movement, Maksut Aşkar is more experimental in his redefinition of traditional Anatolian cuisine. Choose à la carte or the tasting menu and revel in dishes that arrive like small works of edible art. Definitely order something from the wine list, featuring Turkey's best vineyards.

20 **ALAF KURUÇEŞME**
Kuruçeşme Mh.
Kuruçeşme Cd. 19
Beşiktaş ④
+90 532 015 94 19
alafkurucesme.com

With a casual eatery downstairs for lunch and a more upscale Bosphorus-view dining room for dinner upstairs, Alaf is successfully serving up gourmet Turkish street food with the best ingredients such as a venerable *kokoreç* burger.

5 essential spots for STREET FOOD

21 **ŞÖHRETLER BÜFE**
Osmanağa Mh.
Başcavuş Sk. 1
Kadıköy ⑦
+90 216 449 39 36
sohretlerbufe.com

A *büfe* in Istanbul is the place for classic Turkish fast food and Şöhretler is a *büfe* known for its excellent and cheap sandwiches overfilled with delicious (unhealthy) ingredients. Don't be surprised to get a hefty sandwich filled with sausage, fries, melted cheese, *sucuk* (fermented sausage), Russian salad and more.

22 **MEŞHUR UNKAPANI PILAVCISI**
Hacı Kadın Mh.
Atatürk Bulvarı
İMÇ1. blok 1401
Fatih ②
+90 212 522 91 55
unkapanipilavcisi.com

Usually served in a street cart, *tavuk pilav* is a filling portion of buttery rice with chickpeas and chicken breast (plus ketchup). Most famed is the Unkapanı Pilavcısı inside İMÇ (Istanbul Manufacturers Market), a small and casual eatery with framed photos of Turkish celebrities who just love their *tavuk pilav.*

23 **SABIRTAŞI İÇLI KÖFTE**
Asmalı Mescit Mh.
İstiklal Cd. 112
Beyoğlu ①
+90 212 244 82 26
sabirtasi.com.tr

The Sabırtaşı street cart has become an essential part of busy İstiklal Caddesi, but you can also head to the Sabırtaşı restaurant to enjoy the famous *içli köfte*, a crispy bulgur shell filled with fragrant minced meat with walnuts. Make sure to try the other delicious dishes, such as *mantı.*

24 OZZIE'S KOKOREÇ

Asmalımescit Mh.
General Yazgan
Sk. 3-B
Beyoğlu ①
+90 212 361 91 23
ozzieskokorec.com

Kokoreç is definitely an acquired taste and a street food classic preferred after a long night out on the town. At Ozzie's, however, you'll get the sandwich filled with grilled lamb intestines and herbs at its highest and most delicious quality.

25 GÜLEBRU KANTIN

AT: GRAND BAZAAR
Acı Çeşme Sk. 4
Fatih ②
+90 212 512 33 93

This tiny vendor in the often daunting labyrinthine streets of the Grand Bazaar serves some of the best *döner* in town. Catch one of the few seats and order a *dürüm* (wrap with döner meat) and *ayran* (yoghurt drink) and enjoy your fantastic meal while shoppers from all over the world rush by on their consumerist journeys.

23 SABIRTAŞI İÇLI KÖFTE

5 places for the ultimate
TURKISH BREAKFAST

26 **KAHVE 6**
**Kılıçali Paşa Mh.
Anahtar Sk. 13-A
Beyoğlu ①
+90 212 293 08 49
*kahve6.business.site***

Enjoy a full Turkish breakfast spread made from entirely natural ingredients at this very down-to-earth cafe that's a favourite hangout among Cihangir residents. Kahve 6 is also quite the refuge with its botanic pebble garden in the back, decorated with potted plants and a bamboo roof and open all year round.

27 **YENIKÖY KAHVESI**
**Yeniköy Mh.
Kürkçü Faik Sk. 4
Sarıyer ⑥
+90 212 299 38 10
*yenikoykahvesi.com***

After walking up the lovely cobblestoned and verdant Kürkçü Faik Street, Yeniköy Kahvesi appears like a small haven with simple wooden chairs and tables underneath the vines. The special organic Turkish breakfast includes natural olives and honey from Datça, seasonal tomatoes and cucumbers, cheese and jam varieties, eggs and butter.

28 **MINVAL**
Akatlar Mh.
Yaren Sk. 6/12
Beşiktaş ④
+90 212 352 54 70
minval.ist

Dedicated to organic, locavore and artisanal food production, Minval is a cafe that serves freshly made baked goods, pastries and seasonal dishes created by chef Zeynep Karahan herself. The traditional Turkish breakfast is updated with various omelette creations with seasonal fillings, homemade sausage, herbal teas and slices of divine sourdough bread or *simit*.

29 **CLUB MAVI BÜYÜKADA**
Büyüktur Yolu 24
Büyükada ⑧
+90 216 382 60 75
buyukadamavi.com

Istanbul's largest island is also sadly one of its most popular (crowded). That's why Club Mavi is a true blessing with its quiet garden and simple tables overlooking the blue sea. Order the traditional Turkish breakfast and dig into a spread of cheeses, olives, fried eggs, dried fruits, homemade pastries and much more.

30 **ÇAKMAK KAHVALTI SALONU**
Sinanpaşa Mh.
Çelebioğlu Sk. 8
Beşiktaş ③
+90 212 227 04 85

In one corner of the Beşiktaş neighbourhood you'll find Turkish breakfast-only restaurants that become jam-packed on the weekends with hungry locals. Çakmak is the best among them and serves up the full traditional Turkish breakfast, plus *pişi* (fried dough best enjoyed with jam).

5 great places for the MEYHANE (Turkish tavern) EXPERIENCE

31 **SAFA MEYHANESI**
Yedikule Mh.
İlyasbey Cd. 169
Fatih ②
+90 212 585 55 94
tarihisafa meyhanesi.com

An ornate antique chandelier decorates this classic Turkish tavern that has been around for more than 100 years. Safa abides to Istanbul's traditional *meyhane* experience: drinking *rakı*, eating meze, and allowing good conversation to unfurl for hours. Take your pick from the tray of meze and order a bottle of Kulüp Rakı, the house favourite.

32 **BALAT SAHIL RESTORAN**
Balat Mh.
Mürselpaşa Cd. 245
Fatih ②
+90 212 525 61 85

Still very much a local secret, Balat Sahil Restaurant is known for its very antique atmosphere and excellent (yet affordable) dishes. Enjoy meze like *fava* (mashed broad beans), stuffed onion or sautéed liver and the city's best grilled turbot.

33 **MA'NA**
Kemankeş Mh.
Rıhtım Cd. 53-8
Beyoğlu ①
+90 212 293 09 93
karakoymana.com

Inspired by the nostalgic *meyhane* (taverns) of Istanbul, Ma'Na feels as if it has been in the Karaköy neighbourhood forever. With a more modern approach in terms of décor, the menu only features classic cold and warm meze (appetizers), to be shared and enjoyed with many glasses of ice-cold *rakı*.

34 MADAM DESPINA'NIN MEYHANESI

Feriköy Mh.
Açıkyol Sk. 9
Şişli ③
+90 212 247 33 57

Madam Despina was the first woman in Turkey to open a classic tavern and her namesake *meyhane* is still a neighbourhood favourite. Not much has changed here since 1945, including sporadic live *fasıl* music and her classic meze dishes, most notably, *topik*, an Armenian recipe made with chickpeas, onions, nuts, currants, and tahini.

35 KÖR AGOP

Şehsuvar Bey Mh.
Ördekli Bakkal Sk. 7
Fatih ②
+90 212 517 23 34
koragop.com

The Kumkapı quarter is known for its rowdy taverns and street musicians and Kör Agop is the most famous. Established in 1938 by the fisherman Agop, the tavern is now run by the family's third generation who continue to serve their grandmother's famous fish soup. Make sure to also ask about the day's freshest catch.

32 BALAT SAHIL RESTORAN

5 of the city's finest

FINE DINING

36 **MSA RESTAURANT**
Emirgan Mh.
Sakıp Sabancı Cd. 42
Sarıyer ⑥
+90 212 323 30 30
msaninrestorani.com

Located inside the beautiful Sakıp Sabancı Museum, MSA's terrace looks out over the former estate's large garden and the Bosphorus. Run by the students of the city's most important culinary school, you'll find innovative dishes from popcorn shrimp to the perfect lamb tenderloin, or an unforgettable chocolate soufflé.

36 MSA RESTAURANT

37 ALANCHA

AT: MAÇKA KEMPINSKY RESIDENCE
Visnezade Mh.
Şehit Mehmet Sk. 9
Şişli ③
+90 212 261 35 35
alancha.com

Every night, head chef Kemal Can Yurttaş takes diners on a journey through Anatolia's history and regions with experimental tasting menus that redefine local favourites. In the dimly lit minimalistic dining room, a Scandinavian influence is quite apparent, while downstairs the à la carte restaurant and bar are a bit more casual.

38 NICOLE

Tomtom Mh.
Tomtom Kaptan Sk. 18
Beyoğlu ①
+90 212 292 44 67
nicole.com.tr

When chef Aylin Yazıcıoğlu left Cambridge University to pursue her real passion, she ended up studying at École Le Cordon Bleu and working alongside Michelin starred chefs. At her own restaurant, fantastic seasonal tasting menus are accompanied by local chateau-style wines.

39 ANTICA LOCANDA

Arnavutköy Mh.
Satış Meydanı 12
Beşiktaş ④
+90 212 287 97 45
anticalocanda.com.tr

One of the city's only authentic Italian restaurants is run by Milanese Chef Gian Carlo Talerico who presents classic Italian dishes, such as homemade *tagliolini*, with love and in a beautifully upscale dining room and small garden.

40 MIKLA

AT: THE MARMARA PERA
Asmalı Mescit Mh.
Meşrutiyet Cd. 15
Beyoğlu ①
+90 212 293 56 56
miklarestaurant.com

Turkish-Finnish chef Mehmet Gürs coined the 'New Anatolian Kitchen' movement in 2012, and as such Mikla's tasting menu is the product of research and creativity as ingredients from all over Turkey are respectfully reinterpreted. Apart from its gorgeous dining room and bar overlooking the whole city, Mikla also has a summer-only rooftop bar.

5 of the best

CHEAP EATS

41 **LADES**

Katip Mustafa Çelebi Mh. Sadri Alışık Sk. 14-A Beyoğlu ①
+90 212 251 32 03
lades.com.tr

A Beyoğlu classic for cheap but truly delicious lunch fare, Lades regulars know exactly what's served on which day and arrive for that special serving of comforting consistency. Try their amazing *döner* served over buttery rice, *kuzu tandır* (oven-roasted baby lamb) and definitely leave room for dessert.

42 **MUTFAK DILI**

Arap Cami Mh. Ziyalı Sk. 8 Beyoğlu ①
+90 212 254 11 54
mutfakdili.biz

Nestled deep in the maze of hardware stores that make up the other half of Karaköy, Mutfak Dili is where the local shopkeepers go for cheap but delicious lunch specials. Despite becoming quite popular after being featured on TV, Mutfak Dili is still the place for delicious homely Turkish food.

43 DÜRÜMZADE

Hüseyinağa Mh.
Kamer Hatun
Cd. 26-A
Beyoğlu ①
+90 212 249 01 47

You will find plenty of places making *dürüm* in Istanbul, but Dürümzade is just a cut above the rest. The thin *lavaş* bread, which is rubbed with spices, is filled with freshly grilled kebab, onions with sumac, tomatoes and chopped parsley for an all round heavenly wrap.

44 BIZCE ORTAKÖY KURUFASULYECISI

Ortaköy Mh.
Dereboyu Cd. 52
Beşiktaş ③
+90 212 236 06 21
bizcekuru.com

One of Turkey's most popular comfort foods is definitely *kurufasulye pilav* (bean stew with rice) and Bizce is one of the best places to taste this particular comfort. The simple restaurant prepares beans Çayeli-style (a district in the Rize province) with plenty of tomato sauce and beef morsels.

45 BEN-U SEN

Bozkurt Mh.
Baruthane Cd. 37
Şişli ③
+90 212 246 33 26

Hidden away in the residential back-streets of the Kurtuluş area, Ben-u Sen is the place for homecooked dishes, the kind Turkish mothers lovingly cook for their families. Small, cosy and only open for lunch, daily prepared dishes with carefully chosen ingredients are on display including classics such as lentil soup or stuffed grape leaves.

5 *essential* ESNAF LUNCH *restaurants*

46 **NATO LOKANTASI**
Kemankeş Mh.
Karanlık Fırın Sk. 4
Beyoğlu ①
+90 212 249 64 24
natolokantasi.com.tr

An *esnaf lokantası* is a canteen-style lunch spot that serves daily made homey dishes to the neighbourhood's hard-working women and men, and NATO Lokantası has been successfully doing this since 1952 (which also happens to be the year that Turkey became a member of said international alliance.)

47 **YANYALI FEHMI LOKANTASI**
Osmanağa Mh.
Yağlıkçı İsmail Sk. 1
Kadıköy ⑦
+90 216 336 33 33
fehmilokantasi.com

It was Fehmi Sönmezler from the Greek town of Yanya who opened this Kadıköy staple in 1919 and the *Yanyalı Köfte* (meatball wrapped in eggplant), his favourite dish, continues to be served today. Of course Yanyalı has much more to offer in its daily display of Turkish classics, from soups to grilled meats, vegetable dishes to milk desserts.

48 ASLAN

Mollafenari Mh.
Vezirhan Cd. 70
Fatih ②
+90 212 513 76 10

There are only a few venues serving authentic Turkish food far away from the trodden touristic culinary paths and Aslan is definitely one of them. Walk up the stairs to enter the simply elegant dining room and choose your classic Turkish dishes from the display before taking a seat by the window.

49 KANAAT LOKANTASI

Sultantepe Mh.
Selmani Pak Cd. 9
Üsküdar ⑤
+90 216 553 37 91
kanaatlokantasi.com.tr

Open since 1933, Kanaat has become a culinary establishment in Üsküdar, a kind of patriarch among Istanbul's *esnaf lokantaları*. With a décor that hasn't changed much since the 1950s, Kanaat's food is consistently delicious, which is why its regulars come here on a daily basis.

50 ŞAHIN LOKANTASI

Asmalı Mescit Mh.
Orhan Adlı Apaydın Sk. 11-A
Beyoğlu ①
+90 212 244 25 43

Veer away from the chaotic hustle that calls itself İstiklal Caddesi and walk into Şahin Lokantası, the area's trustworthy *esnaf* where the food is always delicious. Open since 1967, lunchtime at Şahin is always a well-choreographed hustle of waiters and head chef, expertly serving up orders that seem to fly to each table.

5 spots for NON-TOURISTY FOOD IN TOURISTY SULTANAHMET

51 **LOKANTA 1741**
AT: ÇAĞALOĞLU HAMAM
Alemdar Mh.
Profesör Kazım
İsmail Gürkan Cd. 34
Fatih ②
+90 533 145 17 41
lokanta1741.com

On the terrace of the historic Çağaloğlu Hamam, this fine dining Turkish restaurant certainly has a very unique location and is one of the few places in the Old City serving up great cocktails. Dine on traditional Turkish dishes with a modern twist made with locally sourced ingredients.

52 **KARIŞMA SEN**
Cankurtaran Mh.
Kennedy Cd. 10
Fatih ②
+90 212 458 00 81
karismasen.com

Once a *gazino* (restaurant with live music) that was favoured by local celebrities, Karışma Sen may no longer have a stage, but the seafood is still excellent. With a view of the Bosphorus and a breezy terrace in the summer, freshly prepared Greek and Turkish meze varieties and seafood are accompanied by ice-cold glasses of *rakı*.

53 **AHIRKAPI BALIKÇISI**

Sultan Ahmet Mh.
Keresteci Hakkı
Sk. 38
Fatih ②
+90 212 518 49 88

This small restaurant only has a few tables and a very casual vibe, but you'll always have a hard time finding a spot because its delicious grilled fish is a favourite among locals. Order a cold glass of beer with your meal and enjoy an authentic Istanbul moment.

54 **GIRITLI**

Cankurtaran Mh.
Keresteci Hakkı Sk.
Fatih ②
+90 212 458 22 70
giritlirestoran.com

In a garden far away from the crowds under the vines and colourful light bulbs, Giritli presents authentic Cretan meze varieties that are as delicious as they are unique. The prix-fixe menu comes with unlimited local alcoholic beverages and at least 15 meze dishes, hot starters, main course and dessert.

55 **EROL LOKANTASI**

Alemdar Mh.
Çatalçeşme Sk. 3
Fatih ②
+90 212 511 03 22

This traditional tradesman restaurant is like a breath of fresh air among all the tourist magnets, especially because Erol Bey still prepares his seasonal dishes fresh and on a daily basis. Open since 1972, the Turkish homecooked dishes are humble in their excellence.

5 places to enjoy
SEAFOOD BY THE BOSPHORUS

56 **JASH BALIK KINALIADA**
Kınalıada Mh.
Alsancak Cd. 27
Adalar ⑧
+90 216 381 44 32
jashistanbul.com

Jash is already a well-known Armenian-Turkish tavern in Cihangir, but its second branch on the Princes Island of Kınalıada is just marvellous. Right by the water close to the ferry port, this restaurant is like a small vacation from the city with a whole array of delicious meze, fresh fish and *rakı*.

57 **KANDILLI SUNA'NIN YERI**
Kandilli Mh.
Kandilli İskele Cd. 4-17
Üsküdar ④
+90 216 332 32 41

The simple wooden tables and chairs of Suna'nın Yeri (Suna's Place) in Kandilli are mere steps away from the Bosphorus. Watch the sunset reflect in the water as you enjoy simple (but delicious) meze and grilled fish. A great place for a romantic date, make sure to try the *kalamar tava* (fried calamari).

58 **BEBEK BALIKÇI**
Bebek Mh.
Cevdet Paşa Cd. 26-A
Beşiktaş ④
+90 212 263 34 47
bebekbalikci.com

This elegant seafood restaurant is right on the Bosphorus and caters to the neighbourhood's well-heeled locals who dine on classic meze dishes and grilled fish while their *rakı* glasses are refilled. In the summer, the windows are pushed back to let in the sea breeze and endless views.

59 İSMET BABA

Kuzguncuk Mh.
Kuzguncuk Çarşı
Cd. 1-A
Üsküdar ⑤
+90 216 553 12 32
ismetbaba.com.tr

Open since 1950 and named in memory of İsmet Dökmecier (whose grandsons now run the business), İsmet Baba is an extension of Kuzguncuk, one of the few Istanbul neighbourhoods that remains true to its historic roots. Look out over the Bosphorus and order meze, fresh fish and plenty of *rakı*.

60 RUMELIHISARI İSKELE RESTAURANT

Rumeli Hisarı Mh.
Yahya Kemal Cd. 1
Sarıyer ⑥
+90 212 263 29 97
rumelihisariiskele.com

Another classic seafood restaurant right on the Bosphorus, İskele Restaurant is located in what used to be the Rumelihisarı ferry dock. With an unobstructed view of the famous strait (thanks to windows all around the elegant dining room), delicious meze and seafood are especially enjoyable during sunsets.

57 KANDILLI SUNA'NIN YERI

5 places for
SPECIALITY FOOD
shopping

61 **KÜRŞAT OLIVE OIL**
Teşvikiye Mh.
Şakayık Sk. 75-B
Şişli ③
+90 212 247 30 31
kursat.com.tr

Hands down the best olive oil you can buy in Istanbul, the Kürşat family mill is in Ayvalık where their olives are cultivated in ancestral groves and produced according to eco-friendly practices. Every olive is hand-picked to avoid bruising the fruit, something you can definitely taste in their fantastically fragrant oil varieties, especially the unfiltered kind.

62 ASRI TURŞUCU

62 ASRI TURŞUCU

Kuloğlu Mh.
Ağa Hamam Cd. 9-A
Beyoğlu ①
+90 212 244 47 24
asritursucu.com

Rows and rows of colourful jars of pickled vegetables decorate this shop in the bohemian Cihangir quarter. Locals come here to buy pickled cabbage, tomatoes, peppers, gherkins or carrots by the kilo, and to drink the very delectable pickle juice that ranges from non- to very spicy.

63 NURI TOPLAR

Tahtakale Mh.
Hasırcılar Cd. 17
Fatih ②
+90 212 522 07 28
kurukahveci nuritoplar.com

Open since 1890, this small shop hidden away in the bustling streets of Tahtakale has the best Turkish coffee in Istanbul. Run by the third generation of the same family, coffee beans are roasted by wood fire and finely ground with a stone mill, all of which imbues the coffee with its unique taste.

64 ANTRE GOURMET

Cihangir Mh.
Bakraç Sk. 14
Beyoğlu ①
+90 212 292 8972
antregourmet.com

A heaven for charcuterie lovers, Antre Gourmet is like an edible museum of regional Turkish cheeses. All cheeses come from their respective regions and only from small family producers who adhere to traditional and organic techniques. If you're feeling peckish, Antre also makes excellent takeaway sandwiches.

65 BÜNSA BAHARAT

Hüseyinağa Mh.
Dudu Odaları Sk. 12-A
Beyoğlu ①
+90 212 243 62 65

Founded by five brothers, whose initials compose the name 'Bünsa', this traditional spice shop might as well be a visual flavour encyclopedia. The many colourful glass jars have everything from curry powder to saffron, as well as teas, pastes and natural beauty products.

The 5 best
BRUNCH SPOTS

66 **BACKYARD**
Bebek Mh.
Bebeköy Sk. 4
Beşiktaş ④
+90 532 131 74 04
backyard.com.tr

One of the only places in Istanbul where you can relax in a garden from breakfast to evening cocktails, Backyard is especially popular for its weekend brunch. Whether you're in the mood for Eggs Benedict, pancakes, a toasted sandwich with prosciutto and mozzarella or just granola with fresh fruits, Backyard has something for every preference.

67 **MANGERIE**
Küçükbebek Mh.
Cevdet Paşa Cd. 69
Beşiktaş ④
+90 212 263 51 99
mangeriebebek.com

Try to snag a table on the balcony for one of Istanbul's best brunches with a beautiful view of the Bosphorus. The menu has everything covered from scrambled eggs with crispy bacon to pancakes with fresh fruits and maple syrup. For something a little more Turkish try the Mangerie Breakfast spread.

68 **DÜN**
Caferağa Mh.
Lütfü Bey Sk. 42-6
Kadıköy ⑦
+90 216 969 63 58

A testament to the fact that healthy and regional food can be downright delicious, Dün not only offers a Turkish breakfast spread, but also omelettes, sourdough bread with hearty toppings and home-made granola with organic honey.

69 NAAN BAKESHOP

Caferağa Mh.
Moda Cd. 113
Kadıköy ⑦
+90 850 221 70 99

Inside a lovely space where natural wood meets terrazzo floor and sea foam green details, Naan Bakeshop is known for its excellent homemade sourdough bread varieties. The cafe and bakery's breakfast traverses delicious bagel sandwiches, eggs of every style, French toast and the classic Turkish breakfast spread.

70 JOURNEY

Kiliçali Paşa Mh.
Akarsu Cd. 21-A
Beyoğlu ①
+90 212 244 89 89
journeycihangir.com

With its vintage furniture and comfy reading corner upstairs, Journey is the perfect cafe to linger for hours. Whether you're in the mood for scones with homemade jams, a farm egg omelette with fresh herbs or organic buckwheat pancakes, Journey has all your brunching needs covered.

69 NAAN BAKESHOP

5 TURKISH FOOD CLASSICS
(and where to eat them)

71 **PIDE**
AT: TATBAK
Nişantaşı Mh.
Akkavak Sk. 38-B
Şişli ③
+90 212 246 13 06
tatbak.com

Pide can best be described as boat-shaped flatbread with different fillings that's baked to crispy perfection. Open since 1960, Tatbak is known for its kebab, however its *pide* varieties are a true sideshow delight with fillings such as *sucuk* (Turkish fermented sausage), melted *kaşar* cheese and minced meat.

72 **LAHMACUN**
AT: HALIL
Caferağa Mh.
Güneşli Bahçe Sk. 26
Kadıköy ⑦
+90 216 337 01 23

Inside the bustling Kadıköy fish market, Halil only makes one thing (and makes it really well): *lahmacun*. Erringly called a 'Turkish pizza', the perfectly crispy-thin disc of dough topped with fragrant minced meat and spices is so much more. Add some parsley, a spritz of lemon, roll it up and enjoy!

73 **BÜRYAN**
AT: SIIRT ŞEREF BÜRYAN
Zeyrek Mh.
İtfaiye Cd. 4
Fatih ②
+90 212 635 80 85
serefburyan.org

A true delight for carnivores, the Siirt speciality *büryan* is made from whole lamb cooked to utter tenderness in a pit. At Siirt Şeref Büryan the freshly cut cubes of lamb are served simply on flatbread (which soaks up all the delectable fat) and a bit of salt.

74 **BÖREK**
AT: TARIHI YENIKÖY BÖREKÇISI
Yeniköy Mh.
Köybaşı Cd. 82
Sarıyer ⑥
+90 532 282 24 77
tarihiyenikoy borekcisi.com

Börek comes in so many different variations, but put simply, it's thin layers of hand-rolled dough that are filled with different ingredients and baked to golden perfection. At Yeniköy Börekçisi you'll get the best introduction to *börek* in all its forms, whether filled with feta cheese, minced meat or spinach.

75 **MANTI**
AT: KARDEŞIM MANTI
Emirgan Mh.
Doğru Muvakkithane Cd. 14
Sarıyer ⑥
+90 212 229 69 17

Mantı is tiny handmade dumplings that are filled with minced meat, boiled and then topped with a garlic yoghurt tomato sauce and garnished with dried mint and red pepper. Run by a mother and son team, Kardeşim Mantı is like a cosy home that makes the city's best *mantı*.

5 places for super sweet TURKISH CONFECTIONS

76 **ALTAN ŞEKERLEME**
Demirtaş Mh.
Kantarcılar 68
Fatih ②
+90 212 522 59 09
altansekerleme.com

You won't have a hard time finding this sweet shop with rows of colourful candy jars decorating its window display. Established in 1865, Altan is run by the fourth generation of the same family and the shop's interior reflects this authentic nostalgia, as well as the Ottoman-style *halva*, Turkish delight and *akide* hard candies.

77 **ÜÇ YILDIZ ŞEKERLEME**
Hüseyinağa Mh.
Dudu Odaları Sk. 7
Beyoğlu ①
+90 212 293 81 70
ucyildizsekerleme.com

Another nostalgic Turkish candy shop, Üç Yıldız is one of the few survivors of old Beyoğlu, hidden away in the backstreets of the Galatasaray fish market. Apart from excellent Turkish delight (especially the mastic kind) and *akide* candy, Üç Yıldız also has amazing homemade jams.

78 **MEŞHUR BEBEK BADEM EZMESI**
Bebek Mh.
Cevdet Paşa Cd. 53-C
Beşiktaş ④
+90 212 263 59 84

This historic shop in the upscale Bebek neighbourhood has been making excellent *badem ezmesi* (almond paste/ marzipan) since 1904. Get a large box to go and ask for a row of pistachio paste as well, which is also quite delicious and often overlooked.

79 ALI MUHIDDIN HACI BEKIR

Hobyar Mh.
Hamidiye Cd. 81-83
Fatih ②
+90 212 522 06 66
hacibekir.com

Ali Muhiddin Hacı Bekir is a tourist favourite when it comes to *lokum* (Turkish delight), but only a few head to Eminönü to visit its original shop, which hasn't changed much since opening in 1777. Take in the nostalgia and get a mixed bag of *akide* candies and some Turkish delight to take home.

80 ŞEKERCI CAFER EROL

Osmanağa Mh.
Yasa Cd. 19
Kadıköy ⑦
+90 216 337 11 03
sekercicafererol.com

The Asian Side's historic candy shop has been around since 1807 and its overtly saccharine Ottoman tastes have remained virtually unchanged. Apart from more than thirty kinds of *lokum* and *akide* candy, Erol also serves traditional desserts such as *bademli şam tatlısı* (a semolina almond cake soaked in syrup).

79 ALI MUHIDDIN HACI BEKIR

5 tasty spots for
VEGETARIANS

81 **BI NEVI DELI**
Etiler Mh.
Dilhayat Sk. 10/1
Beşiktaş ④
+90 212 358 60 32
binevideli.com

Opened by Belkıs Boyacıgiller and Özge Şen in 2014, this deli and bakery is all about the creation of delicious and nourishing dishes from whole, seasonal, plant-based and minimally processed ingredients. Vegetarian and vegan-friendly, there's everything from quinoa muffins to seitan burgers, squash spaghetti and more.

82 **GRAM**
Esentepe Mh.
Büyükdere Cd. 185
Şişli
+90 212 243 10 48
gram.ist

The perfect lunch spot inside the sleek Kanyon shopping centre, Gram is all about regional and seasonal food. Pick from daily vegetarian-friendly options such as Brussels sprout pomegranate seed salad, black-eyed peas with ginger and butternut squash or zucchini fritters.

83 **VI COFFEE & HEALTHY LIVING**
Teşvikiye Mh.
Ahmet Fetgari Sk. 18-B
Şişli ③
+90 212 247 18 37

This cosy neighbourhood cafe is also the ideal lunch spot for vegetarian and vegan fare that focusses specifically on a healthy lifestyle. Vegan pumpkin soup, vegetarian sandwiches and bowls, gluten-free pancakes and brownies, and sugar-free smoothies are all part of the menu. Let's not forget the excellent coffee.

84 ZENCEFIL

Şehit Muhtar Mh.
Kurabiye Sk. 8-10
Beyoğlu ①
+90 212 243 82 34

One of Istanbul's first vegetarian restaurants, Zencefil continues to lift spirits with its colourful walls, ornate tile flooring and beautiful garden filled with blooming potted plants and flowers. The daily specials always include creative homemade vegetarian dishes inspired by the seasons, unique lemonades and delicious desserts such as the famous Zencefil-style pumpkin pie.

85 GALATA KITCHEN

Müeyyetzade Mh.
Tatar Beyi Sk. 9-B
Beyoğlu ①
+90 212 252 20 22

Every dish at Galata Kitchen is prepared by the loving hands of two mothers who spend hours in the kitchen preparing meals composed solely of seasonal produce brought in from local food purveyors. Vegetarians will rejoice at the vegetable-based dishes such as stuffed peppers, eggplant with basil, lentil meatballs and chickpeas with mustard sauce.

85 GALATA KITCHEN

The 5 best places to enjoy
NON-TURKISH FOOD

86 **SMELT & CO**
Balat Mh.
Kiremit Cd. 16-A
Fatih ②
+90 538 286 54 65
smeltandco.com

Chef and owner Sinan Bakkaloğlu worked at Copenhagen's legendary Noma restaurant before he decided to return to Istanbul and open his own place. The frequently updated menu is a confluence of seasonal ingredients heightened by innovative techniques. On the weekends, breakfast is served with homemade cheeses and jams, while dessert is always divine.

87 **MITTAG**
Reşitpaşa Mh.
Kongre Cd. 63
Sarıyer ⑥
+90 212 323 61 25
mittagistanbul.com

You would never think of seeing Mittag in the Reşitpaşa neighbourhood, a not-yet gentrified residential area where simple houses still have fruit trees in their gardens. The modern eatery is chef Fatma Yıldırım's culinary playground where she experiments with seasonal ingredients to create unique dishes such as sesame chicken schnitzel or Phanaeng curry shrimp.

88 **ORORO SUSHI BAR**
Caferağa Mh.
Fırıldak Sk. 14-17
Kadıköy ⑦
+90 216 345 01 81
ororo-sushi.com

A real standout in the Moda area, watch the chef prepare classic and special Nigiri and Sashimi rolls in the open kitchen and make sure to try the Matcha Bites (with matcha and white chocolate) for dessert.

89 **PERA THAI**
Evliya Çelebi Mh.
Meşrutiyet Cd. 94-A
Beyoğlu ①
+90 212 245 57 25
perathai.com

Istanbul's oldest Thai restaurant has been serving the city's most authentic and traditional delicacies since 2001. In a modern dining room with traditional décor touches, authentic dishes such as homemade curries and Pad Thai are prepared by Thai cooks and served in ornamental ceramic tableware.

90 **ÇUKURCUMA 49**
Kuloğlu Mh.
Turnacıbaşı Cd. 49-A
Beyoğlu ①
+90 212 249 00 48

Hidden in the antique-shop quarter of Çukurcuma, Çukurcuma 49 stands out with its exposed brick walls, framed drawings of animals and a wine cellar visible through the glass flooring. The cool restaurant also serves the city's best pizza accompanied by the delicious house wine.

86 SMELT & CO

5 *must-try*
TURKISH DESSERTS

91 **BAKLAVA**
AT: GAZIANTEPLI BAKLAVACI BILGEOĞLU
Cafarağa Mh.
Bahariye Nailbey Sk. 1-B
Kadıköy ⑦
+90 216 336 75 54

Skip the tourist-filled *baklava* purveyors all around Istanbul and seek out this small shop in the Kadıköy neighbourhood for the best *baklava* (plus other classic desserts). Bilgeoğlu hails from Gaziantep, the Turkish *baklava* capital, and makes the dessert with homemade butter, which gives it that exceptional taste.

92 **AYVA TATLISI**
AT: SAKARYA TATLICISI
Hüseyinağa Mh.
Dudu Odaları Sk. 3
Beyoğlu ①
+90 212 249 24 69

The *Ayva Tatlısı* dessert is made by boiling quince with cloves and then soaking it in sweet syrup with a dollop of clotted cream. Head to Sakarya Tatlıcısı to eat the best version of *Ayva Tatlısı* available in Istanbul (or any other Turkish dessert if quince is not really your thing).

93 **ICE CREAM**
AT: DAMLA DONDURMA
Feriköy Mh.
Kurtuluş Cd. 110-A
Şişli ③
+90 212 233 49 25
damladondurma.com

Open since 1989, this small ice-cream shop hasn't changed one bit over the years and makes locals travel back to their childhoods with every scoop that's served on old-school ice-cream cones. Damla's eleven flavours are all beyond excellent, but the *Damla Sakızı* (mastic) is a favourite.

94 **PROFITEROL**
AT: NAZAR PASTANESI
Feriköy Mh.
Kurtuluş Cd. 182-B
Şişli ③
+90 212 225 27 46
kurtulusnazar profiterol.com

Profiterole is not a Turkish dessert per se, but as a city whose history is defined by the confluence of many cultures, the Turkish profiterol is a staple at Istanbul patisseries. The profiterol at Nazar Pastanesi is simply the best, melding together a sweet pastry shell and cream with rich chocolate sauce oh so perfectly.

95 **TAVUKGÖĞSU**
AT: ÖZKONAK MUHALLEBICISI
Kılıçali Paşa Mh.
Akarsu Cd. 46-B
Beyoğlu ①
+90 212 249 13 07

Don't be daunted by the fact that this Turkish milk dessert contains thinly shredded chicken breast; it's very delicious! And the best place to try it is at Özkonak Muhallebicisi, which also happens to be a very classic *esnaf* restaurant serving excellent Turkish homecooked-style dishes.

The 5 best

TURKISH PATISSERIES

96 **BALTEPE PASTANESI**
**Atikali Mh.
Müstakimzade Sk. 33
Fatih ②
+90 212 521 66 56
*baltepe.com.tr***

Open since 1956, this patisserie claims to have been the first to introduce the *trileçe* dessert (a cake soaked in three kinds of milk) to Turkish consumers. However, Baltepe has much more on offer except its famous *trileçe*, so make sure to try their ice creams, Turkish desserts and *kuru pasta* (savoury baked goods).

97 **TARIHI SAVOY PASTANESI**
**Cihangir Mh.
Sıraselviler Cd. 91-A
Beyoğlu ①
+90 212 249 18 18
*savoypastanesi.com***

A true establishment in the Cihangir neighbourhood, Savoy Pastanesi has been open since 1950 consistently serving excellent sweet and savoury goods to locals and visitors alike. Their desserts are especially notable, including favourites such as chocolate eclairs, strawberry tarts and millefeuille with raspberry.

98 İNCI PASTANESI

**Şehit Muhtar Mh.
Mis Sk. 18-A
Beyoğlu ①
+90 212 293 92 24**

Many Istanbul locals were furious when İnci was forcibly removed from its original spot where it had been serving its famous profiteroles since 1944. However, the Beyoğlu landmark thankfully reopened in a new location and continues to make its fantastic pastries and desserts.

99 BAYLAN PASTANESI

**Caferağa Mh.
Muvakkıthane
Cd. 9-A
Kadıköy ⑦
+90 216 346 63 50
*baylangida.com***

Established in 1923, Istanbul's oldest patisserie is as old as the Turkish Republic itself. Baylan's original Kadıköy branch has been around since 1961 and offers a nostalgic world of mouth-watering pastries and desserts. Most famous is the *Kup Griye*, a sundae with vanilla and caramel ice cream and a rich caramel sauce with pieces of almond croquant.

100 ÇENGELKÖY SEVAL PASTANESI

**Çengelköy Mh.
Çengelköy Cd. 9
Üsküdar ④
+90 216 321 55 46
*sevalpastanesi.com***

Another classic Turkish patisserie that's been around since 1957, Seval prides itself on not using any additives in its delicious sweet and savoury pastries as well as desserts. Delicious milk desserts are served with a scoop of their own ice cream and the macarons are some of the best in Istanbul.

5 places to eat
GREAT KÖFTE

101 **KÖFTECI HÜSEYIN**
Şehit Muhtar Mh.
Kurabiye Sk. 9-A
Beyoğlu ①
+90 212 243 76 37

More than forty years ago, Köfteci Hüseyin sold some of the city's best *köfte* from a simple pushcart grill. Even though the cart was traded in for a small eatery, the *köfte* has remained the same and a steady stream of hungry Istanbul locals come here to get their fill of excellent grilled meatballs for lunch.

102 **NAMLI RUMELI KÖFTECISI**
Hocapaşa Mh.
Hocapaşa Sk. 9-11
Fatih ②
+90 212 511 21 96
namlirumeli koftecisi.com

It's said that the Namlı Rumeli Köftecisi doesn't close until he runs out of meatballs. And so locals come to his tiny eatery, ordering portions of *köfte* and *shish* (which is also very good), and leaving just enough space for the amazing dessert: *Irmik Helvası* (semolina halva).

103 **KÖFTECI ALI BABA**
Arnavutköy Mh.
Beyazgül Cd. 2
Beşiktaş ④
+90 212 265 36 12
koftecialibaba.net

Open since the 1980s, Ali Baba is an established Arnavutköy neighbourhood resident with only a few tables serving up delicious grilled *köfte* and *piyaz* (a white bean onion salad with vinaigrette). Whether for lunch or as a late night snack, the *köfte* is always excellent.

104 ÇANAK MANGALDA KURUFASULYE

Balat Mh.
Ayvansaray Cd. 25
Fatih ②
+90 212 621 58 35
mangaldafasulye.com

A lot of people who visit the very photogenic Balat neighbourhood never venture far enough to discover this restaurant that appears rather unremarkable but actually serves some of the best grilled *köfte* and *kurufasulye* (bean stew) in Istanbul. Make sure to try the *manda yoğurdu* (yoghurt from water buffalo milk).

105 KÖFTECI ARNAVUT

Balat Mh.
Mürselpaşa Cd. 139
Fatih ②
+90 212 531 66 52

This small corner eatery has been in the family for generations loyally grilling some of the city's best *köfte* and presenting it with an accompaniment of equally excellent *piyaz*. Leave room for the *Kıbrıs Tatlısı* for dessert, a kind of walnut and coconut cake topped with sweet cream.

105 KÖFTECI ARNAVUT

5 *excellent*

FISH MARKETS

106 KADIKÖY FISHERMEN'S MARKET

Caferağa Mh.
Along Güneşli Bahçe Sk.
Kadıköy ⑦

You'll be able to find much more than fresh fish displayed in all its many glistening variations at the Kadıköy Market. From offal to pickles, coffee to dried fruits and nuts, ready-made meze dishes, honey, cheeses, olives and coffee, the market's many vendors and shops offer everything imaginable.

107 GALATASARAY FISH MARKET

Hüseyinağa Mh.
Along Sahne Sk.
Beyoğlu ①

Located right across the illustrious Galatasaray High School, the Galatasaray Fish Market may have its share of fresh fish on display but also offers much more. From shops specialising in smoked bonito, spices, and Turkish sweets, to vendors selling fresh produce and pickles, this market is preferable for its central location.

108 BEŞIKTAŞ FISH MARKET

Sinanpaşa Mh.
Along Mumcu Bakkal Sk.
Beşiktaş ③

Istanbul's other famous fish market is in the Beşiktaş neighbourhood where you'll only see locals doing their daily shopping. Choose from the large array of fresh seafood or, if you'd rather have someone else cook it for you, head to one of the many fish restaurants right behind the market.

109 BEBEK FISH HOUSE

Bebek Mh.
Cevdet Paşa Cd. 57
Beşiktaş ④
+90 212 265 05 36

This fresh seafood vendor in the upscale Bebek neighbourhood has been around since 1967 and is a local secret when it comes to buying fresh seasonal fish. The store's loyal clientele come by frequently to take their pick from among the fresh sea bass, red mullet, grouper, sea bream and turbot.

110 ÜSKÜDAR FISHERMEN'S MARKET

Mimar Sinan Mh.
Along Atlas Sk.
Üsküdar ⑤

Even if you're not planning on buying anything, strolling through this historic fish market is a delight in itself. Watch on as locals do their haggling and shopping amongst the fish vendors and butchers as well as pickle, Turkish candy and charcuterie shops (to name a few).

5 *essential*
TURKISH BAKERIES

111 **FIRIN ARMA**
Bozkurt Mh.
Kurtuluş Cd. 47-A
Şişli ③
+90 212 230 03 86
firinarma.com

You'll always see a line in front of Fırın Arma in the mornings when locals stop by before work to pick up their Turkish breakfast pastries. You'll have a hard time choosing from all the sweet and savoury baked goods, but do try the *ev poğaçası* (a buttery pastry with cheese and shredded carrot).

112 **EVIN UNLU MAMÜLLERI**
Balat Mh.
Vodina Cd. 82
Fatih ②
+90 212 524 86 11

The reason why this particular street in Balat always smells like delectable baked goods is because of Evin, a family bakery that has been around since 1923. Particular favourites are the many varieties of traditional Turkish cookies and crackers that are handmade without additives and are best enjoyed with Turkish tea.

113 **YEDI SEKIZ HASAN PAŞA FIRINI**
Sinanpaşa Mh.
Şehit Asım Cd. 8
Beşiktaş ③
+90 212 261 97 66

A Beşiktaş institution when it comes to baked goods, Yedi Sekiz Hasan Paşa gets its name from the thick-mustachioed Ottoman Pasha whose photo hangs on the bakery's wall. You'll find all manner of traditional Turkish baked goods, but their cinnamon cookies are especially exceptional.

114 GALATA SIMITÇISI

Kemankeş Mh.
Mumhane Cd. 47-A
Beyoğlu ①
+90 212 244 77 75

No talk of baked goods in Istanbul would be complete without *simit*, the savoury ring shaped pastry covered in sesame seeds. Even though *simit* is rather ubiquitous, the Galata Simitçisi *simit* is just better, warm from the oven and crispy, to be bitten into at any time of the day (but always accompanied by Turkish tea).

115 TARIHI KIREÇBURNU

Kireçburnu Mh.
Haydar Aliyev Cd. 48
Sarıyer ⑥
+90 212 262 10 59
kirecburnufirini.com

Far away from the Istanbul most visitors know, the Kireçburnu residential neighbourhood enjoys its unimpeded view of the Bosphorus. Its eponymous bakery has been around since 1957 and makes beyond excellent baked goods, desserts and a breakfast that local residents love to indulge in on the weekends.

114 GALATA SIMITÇISI

COFFEE DEPARTMENT

45 PLACES FOR A DRINK OR TO DANCE THE NIGHT AWAY

5 very trendy
COCKTAIL BARS

116 **ALEXANDRA**
Arnavutköy Mh.
Bebek Arnavutköy
Cd. 50
Beşiktaş ④
+90 212 287 58 48
alexandrabar.com

Located on the crowded main bar street of the upscale Bosphorus neighbourhood of Arnavutköy, Alexandra definitely has one of the most impressive cocktail menus in the city. Inside a renovated historic building, there's an undoubtedly sophisticated feel with a dimly lit mystery. Head to the rooftop to enjoy the view.

117 **SALON CUMA**

117 **SALON CUMA**
Firuzağa Mh.
Çukurcuma Cd. 53-A
Beyoğlu ①
+90 212 293 20 62
cuma.cc

When a secret bar opens up in Çukurcuma (known for its many antique shops) then it's bound to be inspired by the past. Think of Salon Cuma as a speakeasy inspired cocktail bar with dimly lit antique chandeliers, shiny mahogany surfaces, Chesterfield-style vintage leather sofas and classic cocktails served true to imbibing authenticity.

118 **FLEKK**
Galatasaray Mh.
Yeni Çarşı Cd. 54-A
Beyoğlu ①
+90 212 252 80 99

In a narrow and descending cobblestoned street, Flekk is a real neighbourhood cocktail bar with people usually standing outside with their drinks and chatting away. Follow their Instagram account for upcoming DJ parties and enjoy their syrup-free cocktails of great delicious-ness.

119 **FINN KARAKÖY**
Karaköy Mh.
Arapoğlan Sk. 8-B
Beyoğlu ①
+90 530 946 08 88

One of the few bars that has managed to stay open in the Karaköy neighbourhood (which sadly saw its popularity dwindle over the years) Finn will always be strong with its excellent cocktails and finger foods. Onurcan Gençer is the talented mixologist who loves the fresh and fruity ingredients that give his cocktails pizzazz.

120 **MARKUS TAVERN**
Firuzağa Mh.
Hayriye Cd. 16
Beyoğlu ①
+90 212 252 26 52
markusribs.com

Restaurant and cafe by day and rampant cocktail bar by night, Istanbul's cool kids really love filling up this bar to capacity, often spilling out into the streets when the weather permits. DJs play on the weekends and dancing is definitely encouraged.

The 5 coolest
NIGHTLIFE SPOTS

121 **KLEIN**
Harbiye Mh.
Cebel Topu Sk. 4
Şişli ③
+90 212 291 84 40

Often referred to as the Berghain of Istanbul, not because of anything lascivious but because of the picky doorman, KLEIN is for people who want to dance carelessly to good electronic music. In the summer, the KLEIN crowd goes to the rooftop club KLEIN.garten on Meşrutiyet Caddesi 67.

122 **BINA**
Caferağa Mh.
Kadife Sk. 26
Kadıköy ⑦
+90 216 330 84 66

With a whole house to itself on Kadife Sokak (Velvet Street – Kadıköy's infamous nightlife epicentre), Bina is a cafe by day, where locals hang out in the comfy lounges upstairs, and a restaurant and bar at night. Listen to different DJs spin their best every week while you mingle with the cool crowd in the courtyard.

123 **MINI MÜZIKHOL**
Cihangir Mh.
Soğancı Sk. 3
Beyoğlu ①
+90 212 245 19 96
minimuzikhol.com

A true Istanbul nightlife institution, all the cool kids end up at Mini when every other bar begins to close. A tiny apartment-turned-club, some of the city's best DJs perform here on the weekends to a carefree crowd that is not yet ready to call it a night.

124 SUMA HAN

Karaköy Mh.
Yanıkkapı Sk. 3
Beyoğlu ①
+90 532 131 20 59
sumaproductions.com

This gorgeous historic apartment building hosts Istanbul's best parties on its lower floor. Seasonal events include a coveted line-up of local and international DJs that infuse the crowd with enough energy to keep them going until the wee hours of the morning. That and the delicious cocktails, of course.

125 MENTHA

Kamer Hatun Mh.
Meşrutiyet Cd. 34
Beyoğlu ①
+90 554 923 40 43
mentha.co

If partying on a rooftop with a 360-degree view of Istanbul is your thing, then make sure to put Mentha on your nightlife list. Some of the best local DJs such as Barış K. play at Mentha, and you'll be happy to know that they also serve delicious food and cocktails.

122 **BINA**

5 *of the best*
PUBS *in Istanbul*

126 **ZEPLIN PUB**
Caferağa Mh.
Moda Cd. 70
Kadıköy ⑦
+90 216 700 20 02
zeplinpub.com

Kadıköy is very fond of the beer-drinking culture with many pubs strewn all around its various neighbourhoods. One of the longstanding favourites is Zeplin and you'll always see people there conversing over beers and enjoying finger foods like honey BBQ chicken wings or onion rings.

127 **CRAFT BEER LAB**
Sinanpaşa Mh.
Şair Nedim Cd. 4
Beşiktaş ③
+90 212 236 91 92

Craft Beer Lab has a few surprises up its sleeve including a very large menu of beers from all over the world, a lot of which you've probably never heard of before. Another welcomed surprise is the pub's lovely garden, the perfect place for beer and snacks in the summer.

128 **KARGA BAR**

Caferağa Mh.
Kadife Sk. 16
Kadıköy ⑦
+90 216 449 17 25
karga.com.tr

Compared to the other bars and clubs on Kadıköy's Velvet Street, Karga is a much more relaxed pub where you can simply lounge around and enjoy a few beers over good conversation. Karga also hosts live music on its stage as well as events such as movie nights or talks with established writers at kargART.

129 **TAPS BEBEK**

Bebek Mh.
Cevdet Paşa Cd. 119
Beşiktaş ④
+90 212 263 87 00
tapsbebek.com

One of the only pubs in Istanbul that's by the Bosphorus, Taps Bebek is a true neighbourhood pub where locals enjoy their beers with a view of the famous strait. Take a stroll by the water on the Bebek boardwalk and watch the sunset with beer and finger foods.

130 **BOSPHORUS BREWING COMPANY**

Esentepe Mh.
Yıldız Posta Cd. 1/1-A
Gayrettepe
+90 212 288 64 99
bosphorus-brewing.com

The only place in Istanbul where you can drink a genuine and locally brewed ale, Bosphorus Brewing Company is an authentic pub and brewery run by Philip and Jill Hall, a couple from Doncaster (UK). Enjoy an Istanbul Pale Ale with fish and chips fried in a special beer batter.

5 bars with
STUNNING VIEWS

131 **SPAGO**
Harbiye Mh.
Mim Kemal Öke Cd. 35
Şişli ③
+90 212 368 08 08
spago.thestregis istanbul.com

On the very posh St. Regis Istanbul hotel rooftop you'll find Spago, master chef Wolfgang Puck's California cuisine restaurant and its gorgeous bar. Order a cocktail and enjoy the view over Istanbul or head to the lounge in case of bad weather for the same amazing views.

132 **GEORGES TERRACE**
AT: GEORGES HOTEL
Müeyyedzade Mh.
Serdar-ı Ekrem Sk. 24
Beyoğlu ①
+90 212 244 24 23
georges.com

Hidden among the lovely boutiques of cobble-stone-bedecked Serdar-ı Ekrem, Georges Hotel occupies a beautiful apartment building from the 1860s. Its rooftop bar and restaurant is the perfect place for a dimly lit evening sipping cocktails and looking out over the city's flickering lights.

133 **BÜYÜK LONDRA OTELI TERRACE BAR**
Asmalı Mescit Mh.
Meşrutiyet Cd. 53
Beyoğlu ①
+90 212 245 06 70
londrahotel.net

Virtually unaltered since its establishment in 1892, during the glamorous days of the Orient Express, the Grand Hotel de Londres has an Ottoman-Victorian elegance with plenty of red velvet. Apart from the bar downstairs with its caged exotic birds, the hotel also has a terrace bar with a fantastic view of Istanbul.

134 PERÒ

Yeniköy Mh.
Daire Sk. 5
Sarıyer ⑥
+90 212 223 77 77

You'll feel like you can jump into the Bosphorus at any time because of this restaurant and bar's location right on the water. Decked out in marble-top tables and French bistro chairs, there's a sense of sophistication that's also reflected in the seasonal menu and craft cocktails.

135 MONKEY BAR

Evliya Çelebi Mh.
Sadi Konuralp Cd. 5
Beyoğlu ①
+90 212 238 50 50
monkeyistanbul.business.site

Istanbul is truly fortunate to have access to the top of the Deniz Palas Apartment, now used as the headquarters of IKSV (Istanbul Foundation for Culture and Art). Monkey Bar, belonging to Firuze Restaurant, looks out over the Golden Horn in all its splendour, made more enjoyable with a round of delicious cocktails.

135 MONKEY BAR

5 of the best
WINE BARS

136 **SOLERA WINERY**
Tomtom Mh.
Yeni Çarşı Cd. 44
Beyoğlu ①
+90 212 252 27 19

Small and cosy, Solera only has a few wooden tables but plenty of shelving where bottles upon bottles of wines are on display and awaiting to be uncorked. Owner and wine expert Süleyman Er is more than happy to give out recommendations, all of which go very nicely with the daily special or the cheese platter.

137 **SENSUS WINE BOUTIQUE**
Bereketzade Mh.
Büyükhendek Cd. 5
Beyoğlu ①
+90 212 245 56 57
sensuswine.com

Located underneath the Anemon Hotel right by the Galata Tower, Sensus has more than 350 bottles of local wine, quite the introduction to the rapidly growing Turkish wine industry. Pick up a bottle to go or sit down to have a taste accompanied by cheese and fruit.

138 **SUVLA KANYON**
AT: KANYON SHOPPING CENTRE TERRACE
Esentepe Mh.
Büyükdere Cd. 185
Şişli
+90 212 353 54 64
suvlakanyon.com

An award-winning family owned wine producer from Eceabat, Suvla is one of the country's top names in the burgeoning Turkish viticulture scene. At their own wine bar in the modern Kanyon shopping centre you'll find a wide range of their excellent wines to be enjoyed with small delicious snacks.

139 **İNCIRLI ŞARAPHANE**
Kuruçeşme Mh.
Muallim Naci Cd. 107
Beşiktaş ④
+90 212 257 11 29
incirlisaraphane.com

This restored historic winery in Kuruçeşme very befittingly has one of Turkey's largest collections of local wines (650 varieties to be exact). Inform yourself in the 'wine library', have a taste in the cellar accompanied by a large selection of cheeses or reserve a table at the restaurant.

140 **VIKTOR LEVI**
Caferağa Mh.
Damacı Sk. 4
Kadıköy ⑦
+90 216 449 93 29
viktorlevimoda.com

One of Istanbul's oldest wine bars was established by Jewish journalist, publisher and wine entrepreneur Viktor Levi in 1914. Even though the original location changed, the name has stayed the same and nowadays Viktor Levi is a haunt for wine lovers who linger in the venue's lovely garden sipping, eating and conversing.

5 *coffee shops for* CAFFEINE-CONNOISSEURS

141 **MONTAG COFFEE ROASTERS**
Caferağa Mh.
Muvakkithane Cd. 16
Kadıköy ⑦
+90 533 690 47 98
montagcoffee.com

You'd never find Montag unless you were specifically looking for it. Located on the second floor overlooking the busy street below, the roastery and cafe has a sleek brass-wood-marble interior as well as carefully chosen coffee beans from around the world that appeal to every taste.

142 **COFFEE DEPARTMENT**
Ayvansaray Mh.
Kürkçü Çeşmesi Sk. 5
Fatih ②
+90 532 441 66 63
coffeedepartment.co

Balat, Istanbul's old Jewish quarter, is alive with new venues opened by young people who are turning their dreams into reality. Coffee Department is Balat's craft coffee shop with a very serious Probatino coffee roaster and the high-quality brews of owner Metin Benbasat who simply loves what he does.

143 **FOUR LETTER WORD COFFEE**
Burgazada Mh.
Takımağa Meydanı Sk. 3-2
Adalar ⑧
+90 216 381 21 80
4lwcoffee.com

Located on Burgaz island, this little roastery and cafe (only open on the weekends) was established by two childhood friends from Chicago and Istanbul respectively. After enjoying some responsibly sourced and roasted coffee, head to the nearby home-turned-museum of Sait Faik Abasıyanık, one of Turkey's greatest writers.

144 PETRA TOPAĞACI

Teşvikiye Mh.
Orhan Ersek Sk. 18
Şişli ③
+90 212 356 10 53
petracoffee.com

Inspired by New York's speciality coffee scene, Kaan Bergsen amassed roasting knowledge at Toby's Estate in Brooklyn and returned to Istanbul to put his education and passion to practice. The result was Petra, a roasting company and cafe where making excellent coffee and educating consumers about good taste is the sole aim.

145 RAFINE ESPRESSO BAR

Caferağa Mh.
Sarraf Ali Sk. 15
Kadıköy ⑦
+90 535 035 46 35
rafineespressobar.com

Kadıköy's third-wave coffee roastery is spread out comfortably on two floors with plenty of space to work on your laptop or read a book the entire day. Known for their excellent brews, Rafine also prides itself on its homemade baked goods such as Salted Caramel and Chocolate Tart or Cinnamon Rolls.

142 COFFEE DEPARTMENT

5 places to sip
TURKISH TEA

146 **ISTANBUL FERRIES**
From the Kadıköy / Beşiktaş / Eminönü Ferry Stations
+90 212 313 80 00
en.sehirhatlari.istanbul

The historic Istanbul ferry is definitely one of the most nostalgic places to sip on Turkish tea. You'll always find tea brewing at the small kiosk inside every ferry, or waiters walking around with trays of tea and snacks. Take in the view of the Bosphorus and enjoy tea in the traditional tulip shaped glass.

146 ISTANBUL FERRIES

147 TARIHI ÇINARALTI ÇAY BAHÇESI

Çengelköy Mh.
Çınarlı Camii Sk. 4
Üsküdar ④
+90 216 422 10 36
tarihicinaralti.istanbul

You'll find traditional *çay bahçeleri* (tea gardens) all over Turkey, but Istanbul has the good fortune of having waterfront views. Locals like to buy *börek* from the bakery next door and sit in the Tarihi Çınaraltı Çay Bahçesi to enjoy the direct view of the Bosphorus with their Turkish tea.

148 CIHANGIR CIHANNÜMASI

Kılıçali Paşa Mh.
Sanatkarlar Cd.
Beyoğlu ①

When you walk down this particular hidden street in Cihangir, you'll suddenly be facing one of the best views of Istanbul. What used to be a tiny tea corner with a few plastic chairs has been turned into a large Ottoman-style gazebo overlooking the excellent view.

149 MODA AILE ÇAY BAHÇESI

Caferağa Mh.
Park İçi Yolu
Kadıköy ⑦
+90 216 337 99 86

The place for Kadıköy locals to hang out on the weekends, the Moda Aile Çay Bahçesi is as Turkish as it gets. Overlooking the Moda boardwalk, the Bosphorus and the European side, this tea garden is a family-friendly cafe where you can observe local life and enjoy Turkish tea with a view.

150 DOLMABAHÇE KAFETERYA

Vişnezade Mh.
Dolmabahçe Cd. 2
Beşiktaş ③

Not a lot of visitors know about this tea garden that's located right by the famous Dolmabahçe Palace and is just a few steps away from the Bosphorus. On warm days, drinking tea with the ferries gliding by and a fresh sea breeze in your face is absolutely divine.

153 **MELEZ TEA LAB**

The 5 best cafes to
MEET A FRIEND

151 **MÜZ ÇUKURCUMA**
Fıruzağa Mh.
Hayriye Cd. 18-A
Beyoğlu ①
+90 212 243 22 62
muz.se

Succulents in beautiful ceramic pots, geometrical terrariums and lush leafy houseplants all decorate this small oasis in the middle of Beyoğlu. Part botanic store, part cafe, Müz is a great place to sit by the window and converse for hours over coffee and something sweet, and to shop for something green.

152 **COOKLIFE BALAT**
Balat Mh.
Akçin Sk. 3-A
Fatih ②
+90 212 982 15 78
cooklife.com

The cafe belonging to Cooklife Magazine (a quarterly Kinfolk-inspired culinary and lifestyle publication) is just serene in its minimalism. Order a cup of coffee and definitely try one of their freshly made pies or desserts such as cookies with white chocolate, macadamia nuts and cranberries.

153 MELEZ TEA LAB

Reşitpaşa Mh.
Kongre Cd. 81-A
Sarıyer ⑥
+90 212 229 29 69
meleztea.com

Istanbul's first concept tea space is a sleek world of artisanal tea blends and their stories. Inspired by the Japanese wabi-sabi worldview (which focusses on the acceptance of transience and imperfection), the serenity of Melez's interior design invites its visitors to sit down, relax and enjoy something special like a *matcha affogato* or a chai spiced hot chocolate.

154 ŞIMDI

Mescit Mh.
Asmalımescit Cd. 5
Beyoğlu ①
+90 212 252 54 43

Located on the ground floor of a historic apartment building, Şimdi is the perfect neighbourhood cafe where locals meet for coffee or food anytime of the day. Try to catch a seat on the comfy couches by the entrance and linger for hours with a friend, conversing, drinking and eating.

155 YER

Moda Mh.
Ferit Tek Sk. 25-A
Kadıköy ⑦
+90 216 450 16 70

Kadıköy's neighbourhood cafe is utterly charming with its vintage furniture and framed art from local artists. Open all day and serving everything from breakfast to Turkish comfort food to evening cocktails, Yer is the casual spot to hang out with a friend for hours.

The 5 spots for traditional
TURKISH COFFEE

156 **MANDABATMAZ**
Asmalı Mescit Mh.
Olivia Geçidi 1-A
Beyoğlu ①
+90 212 243 77 37
mandabatmaz.com.tr

This tiny coffee shop on a side street off İstiklal has been making perfectly foamy cups of Turkish coffee since 1967. Remember that Turkish coffee is quite strong, so order it *orta* (a bit sweet) or *şekerli* (very sweet) if you're not a fan of bold and bitter coffee.

157 **ETHEM TEZÇAKAR KAHVECI**
AT: GRAND BAZAAR
Halıcılar Cd. 61-63
Fatih ②
+90 212 513 21 33

This small historic cafe in the middle of the rather chaotic Grand Bazaar has been serving up excellent Turkish coffee for four generations. The great taste is due to Tezçakar's preference for the Nuri Toplar brand of Turkish coffee (which you can also buy in the Nuri Toplar shop in the Tahtakale neighbourhood).

158 **LATIFE TÜRK KAHVECISI**

Şahkulu Mh.
Galip Dede Cd. 85
Beyoğlu ①
+90 212 293 55 20
latifekahve.com

A lovely coffee roastery on the descending street toward Galata Tower and decked out in sea foam greens, Latife makes an excellent cup of Turkish coffee, especially with *damla sakızı* (mastic). If you're in the mood for some more caffeine, try their excellent Frappe, the perfect summer refreshment.

159 **BEBEK KAHVE**

Bebek Mh.
Cevdet Paşa Cd. 18
Beşiktaş ④
+90 212 257 54 02
bebekkahve.com.tr

A true local hang-out, Bebek Kahve is a cafe right by the Bosphorus with simple wooden tables and chairs and a whole lot of charm. Locals love to meet their friends here for breakfast on the weekend or just to have a cup of Turkish coffee with a beautiful view of the famous strait.

160 **OKKALI KAHVE**

Sinanpaşa Mh.
Yeni Hamam Sk. 3
Beşiktaş ③
+90 212 236 95 06
okkalikahvem.com

A real Beşiktaş neighbourhood spot for a coffee break, Okkalı has an extensive menu of different types of Turkish coffee. Take your pick from *menengiç* (Turkish coffee made from wild pistachios), *kakuleli* (Turkish coffee with cardamom), *tatar* (Turkish coffee with clotted cream) and more.

158 **LATIFE TÜRK KAHVECISI**

DER-LIEBLING

85 PLACES TO SHOP

5 *gorgeous*
FLOWER SHOPS

161 **MITZA**
Yeniköy Mh.
Yarış Sk. 1
Sarıyer ⑥

This flower shop and atelier fully reflects the sweet benevolence of its florist Çağla Yılmaz who gave up a career in pharmaceuticals to fully dedicate herself to a love of nature. Beautiful cut flowers, dried flowers and potted plants decorate the airy shop as well as handmade design objects from local talent.

162 **VESAIRE**
ŞTeşvikiye Mh.
Ahmet Fetgari Sk. 51-B
Şişli (3)
+90 212 231 87 34
vesaire.me

Ayça Girgin's small shop in Teşvikiye has made big waves since opening in 2012, especially her custom-made bridal bouquets with flowers you won't likely find anywhere else. Every week fresh flowers arrive from Holland and Kenya, and the shop window changes completely, reflecting a very inspiring floral wonderland.

163 FLOW FLORAL LIVING

**Fatih Sultan Mehmet Mh.
Bilgi Sk. 3
Sarıyer ⑥
+90 212 323 10 20
*flowistanbul.com***

In love with flowers since childhood, Burcu Uğur left the corporate world and opened her own shop to focus on her passion for floral design. Her arrangements are always one-of-a-kind and specially made for each customer, whether it's for an event or just a space that is in need of natural colour and beauty.

164 DIRHEM FLOWERS & MORE

**Teşvikiye Mh.
Ahmet Fetgari Sk. 41
Şişli ③
+90 532 680 60 03**

A little paradise of succulents, cacti and potted palms, it seems to always be the height of summer inside this beautiful flower shop and cafe. After doing some shopping, order a coffee and something sweet and relax in the hammock or the comfy seat on the windowsill.

165 MISK

**Reşitpaşa Mh.
Emirgan Sk. 22
Sarıyer ⑥
+90 0212 277 07 75
*miskistanbul.com***

Much more than a flower shop with beautiful bouquets and potted plants, Misk also sells artisan chocolates, candles, and ceramics. Opened by Hazal Şen and Eda Erbilgin, the shop also has a cafe serving croissants and bagel sandwiches as well as healthy bowls and smoothies.

5 shops for unique
WOMEN'S FASHION

166 **TRU.PROJECT**
Bebek Mh.
Küçük Bebek Cd. 14/1
Beşiktaş ④
+90 212 287 77 40
truproject.net

Established by Aysu Akagündüz in 2009, this boutique features super soft T-shirts, sweatshirts, tights, dresses, skirts and athletic wear made from high-quality fabrics that emphasise all the right proportions. The brand's minimal style is also reflected in its store, which has its own coffee shop and bookshop.

167 **A HIDDEN BEE**
Tomtom Mh.
Kumbaracı Yokuşu 30-B
Beyoğlu ①
ahiddenbee.com

A mindful clothing brand created by Aylin Erel in 2017, this store and creative design studio makes beautiful and contemporary garments for women who appreciate authenticity. Every item is made from locally produced fabrics, with a focus on the natural and responsible.

168 **YASEMIN ÖZERI**
Galata Mh.
Galip Dede Cd. 93-B
Beyoğlu ①
+90 212 243 43 64
yaseminozeri.com

This Istanbul-based female designer launched her eponymous brand in 2009 and has since made her mark with timeless collections that definitely prefer the beauty of simplicity. A supporter of handmade and local manufacturing, collections are muted in colour with a Scandinavian spirit.

169 FEY

Harbiye Mh.
Mim Kemal Öke Cd. 9
Şişli ③
+90 212 219 87 24
fey.com.tr

The first person to hold the title of 'fashion editor' in Turkey, you can only imagine what Fatoş Yalın's own boutique looks like. FEY oozes sophistication from its carefully selected vintage items to the pieces from its own collection. One can imagine that Katharine Hepburn would have shopped here.

170 MAPA

Harbiye Mh.
Abdi İpekçi Cd. 22/1
Şişli ③
+90 212 230 80 90
mapa-boutique.com

A family company established in 1969, Mapa offers clothing for women who don't want to dress like everyone else. Collections are created by Mapa's Paris-based designers according to the latest trends and handcrafted by the company's own ateliers in Istanbul. From floral dresses to perfectly tailored coats, Mapa always has standout pieces.

169 FEY

5 shops for unique
MEN'S FASHION

171 **BEY KARAKÖY**
Kemankeş Mh.
Mumhane Cd. 54-1
Beyoğlu ①
+90 532 700 59 55
beykarakoy.com

A men's boutique that not only sells clothing but also a whole lifestyle, Bey Karaköy is the place for people who are quite fond of the Nordic aesthetic and culture. You'll find simple but stylish T-shirts, linen button downs, sweaters, jeans, jackets and accessories as well as magazines such as *Kinfolk* and *Monocle*.

172 **1290 SQM**
AT: ZORLU SHOPPING CENTER
Levazım Mh.
Koru Sk. 2
Beşiktaş ④
+90 212 249 01 21
1290sqm.com

After opening shops in Amsterdam and Zurich, 290sqm unveiled itself as 1290sqm in Istanbul inside the very modern Zorlu Shopping Center. The carefully chosen collection of unique items represents a very distinct understanding of style and feature brands such as A.P.C., Won Hundred, Dagmar, Fjällräven and much more.

173 **WUNDER**
Caferağa Mh.
Hünkar Sk. 4-A
Kadıköy ⑦
+90 216 337 08 77
wunder.com.tr

A wonderland for sneaker-lovers, WUNDER loves to show off their collection of the coolest kicks you can find in Istanbul. Check out classic to specially designed sneakers from Nike, Puma, Asics, Adidas, Vans and Reebok as well as comfy cool clothing and accessories.

174 CIVAN

Müeyyedzade Mh.
Serdar-ı Ekrem Cd. 20,
Braunstein Apt. 2
Beyoğlu ①
+90 543 685 76 57
civanistanbul.com

A fashion house inspired by the nostalgic Istanbul gentleman, Civan is all about the revival of perfect tailoring. Founded by designers Bahar Gözkün and Kerem Küçükgürel in 2012, the shop offers formal and casual wear, beautiful bow and neckties and precious vintage buttons. Individual pieces from the twice-yearly collections can also be custom-made to order.

175 LES BENJAMINS

Teşvikiye Mh.
Akkavak Sk. 16
Şişli ③
+90 212 234 93 05
lesbenjamins.com

Istanbul's own luxury street wear brand founded by Bunyamin Aydın is all about local stories and cultural innuendos manifested in comfortably cool menswear of high craftsmanship. The flagship store reflects the brand's urbanity with raw concrete and glass textures and was designed with the help of environmental architecture studio Food New York.

174 CIVAN

The 5 coolest

CONCEPT STORES

176 **SOUQ DÜKKAN**
AT: KANYON SHOPPING CENTRE
Esentepe Mh.
Büyükdere Cd. 185
Şişli
+90 212 265 11 99
souqdukkan.com

What started out as a weekly bazaar, chock full of pretty items from small independent brands carefully selected by its founder Yaprak Aras, became so successful that it opened its own store. Browse very unique items such as colourful hand-printed silk scarves by Rumisu, gorgeous vintage rarities by Ece Sükan Vintage or handmade ceramics by Bornn.

177 **MAE ZAE**
Kemankeş Mh.
Hoca Tahsin Sk. 16-A
Beyoğlu ①
+90 212 288 77 68
maezae.com

Take the stairs down to this basement loft to browse through gorgeous items selected by its owner Münire Alabaz. Apart from the stylish sunglasses and watches of Swedish brand Triwa (for which Alabaz is the Turkey distributor), you'll also find clothing, jewellery and home accessories from local designers.

178 PUNTA DESIGN

Caferağa Mh.
Damacı Sk. 1-A
Kadıköy ⑦
+90 543 768 00 16
puntadesign.com

The Asian side's favourite concept store is an eye-catching and colourful mélange of handmade items from local designers. From sunglasses to bags, jewellery to decorative pillows, clothing to illustrated phone cases, you'll definitely spend a long time browsing through all the tempting objects.

179 SLOW PUBLIC

Vişnezade Mh.
Süleyman Seba
Cd. 83
Akaretler ③
+90 212 227 09 22
slowpublic.com

A concept store that believes in the power of slowing down and enjoying the moment, you'll never find anything mass-produced at Slow Public. With a preference for local producers and natural materials, you'll definitely be enticed by the store's rather large window display with home decoration, clothing, accessories, textiles and stationary on show.

180 SHOPI GO

Teşvikiye Mh.
Ahmet Fetgari 62
Şişli ③
shopigo.com

Turkey's first and only online concept shop launched in 2012 and soon opened its own store, becoming the go-to place for lovers of contemporary brands and luxury streetwear. Brands such as Comme des Garçons, Marc Jacobs, Veja, Wood Wood and many more await in a two-floor glass and concrete haven.

182 TULU TEXTILES

The 5 best shops for beautiful TEXTILES

181 MEKHANN
Firuzağa Mh.
Boğazkesen Cd. 32-A
Tophane ①
+90 212 249 78 49
mekhann.com

Individually displayed and glowing with rich colours, all of Mekhann's home textiles and tapestries are simply ravishing, offering one of the best opportunities to add something irreplaceable to your home. Hand-embroidered and naturally dyed, all of Mekhann's textiles are meticulously produced whilst abiding strictly to traditional production techniques.

182 TULU TEXTILES
Binbirdirek Mh.
Peykhane Sk. 38 3-7
Fatih ②
+90 212 518 87 10
tulutextiles.com

Elizabeth Hewitt's designs are inspired by every moment, from travelling through Morocco to hearing live music or photographing worn down marble. As the owner of Tulu Textiles, all her colourful fabrics also have their own story to tell, whether it's a Dupatta shawl, a decorative pillow or a whole bedding set.

183 YAZZMA

AT: GRAND BAZAAR
Takkeciler Sk. 48-50
Fatih ②
+90 532 412 81 88

In the Grand Bazaar, a shopping terrain not easily mastered given its labyrinthine streets and what seems like an eternity of shops, Yazzma manages to stand out because of its effusive colours. Admire the traditional *suzani* and *ikat* pillows in bright floral hues as well as the pashminas and kaftans.

184 CHAMPA ISTANBUL

Harbiye Mh.
Abdi Ipekçi Cd. 73
Şişli ③
+90 212 231 32 08
champaturkey.com

Just follow the large sign on the street that leads you to this boutique hidden behind an apartment building. Turning their love for travel into a brand, Ayşe Ataman and Sera Geray import and sell clothing, home textiles and accessories from local designers in India and the Far East.

185 SIVASLI ISTANBUL YAZMACISI

AT: GRAND BAZAAR
Yağlıkcılar Sk. 57
Fatih ②
+90 212 526 77 48

A Grand Bazaar shop that stands out with its authentic and high-quality textiles, Sivaslı Istanbul Yazmacısı is truly a haven of colour and embroidery. You'll find traditional hand-painted, hand-woven or tinsel-thread embroidered fabrics, as well as antique Anatolian garments that have been a source of inspiration for Turkish designers.

5
VINTAGE BOUTIQUES
for great finds

186 **SENTETIK SEZAR**
Cafereğa Mh.
Leylek Sk. 20-B
Kadıköy ⑦
+90 530 775 16 48
sentetiksezar.com

You won't find dusty old garments at this very hip vintage shop where it's all about reviving old trends for a unique personal fashion statement. From overtly floral dresses to laidback plaid shirts, purple cat eye sunglasses to delicate pendant necklaces, Sentetik Sezar has it all (for men and women).

187 **FASHION AT EYE**
Kemankeş Mh.
Franzıs Geçidi Sk. 53
Beyoğlu ①
fashionateye.com

This is the place to buy your next pair of sunglasses and there's plenty to choose from including unworn vintage sunglasses, collections from contemporary and independent designers and handmade pieces. It's no surprise that owner Hakan Şan comes from a family of eyewear experts and is often referred to as the 'Turkish eyewear guru'.

188 RAG'N ROLL VINTAGE

Balat Mh.
Yıldırım Cd. 31-A
Fener ②
+90 536 782 29 15

You'll recognise this small vintage store from the white bike that's standing right outside its shop window. Inside you'll find a lovely collection of vintage leather bags and shoes as well as sunglasses, jewellery and clothing with a strong nostalgic focus on the 1950s and 1960s.

189 BÜYÜKANNEMIN SANDIĞI

Caferağa Mh.
Şair Latifi Sk. 28-B
Kadıköy ⑦
+90 535 408 64 86
buyukannemin sandigi.com

Even though Büyükannemin Sandığı translates to 'My Grandmother's Trunk', you won't find any old lady clothes at this cool vintage boutique. Think vintage Aztec jackets, chunky 1990s sweaters and bomber jackets and long floral dresses that you'll be browsing through and falling in love with.

190 BY RETRO

Asmalı Mescit Mh.
Suriye Pasajı 166-C
Beyoğlu ①
+90 212 245 64 20

You can spend hours in this giant basement shop playing dress up like a kid and travelling back through many different fashion eras. Retro wedding dresses, vintage sailor jackets, puffy costume dresses, fluffy boas, sunhats with ribbons and so much more await to be discovered in this treasure chest of vintage and secondhand.

5 *very non-touristy*
ISTANBUL SOUVENIRS

191 **ARTRIUM**
Şahkulu Mh.
Müellif Sk. 12
Beyoğlu ①
+90 212 251 43 02
artrium.com.tr

Hacer Sayman played an important part in the Beyoğlu neighbourhood's rebirth with her restoration projects in the 1990s and Artrium is her latest endeavour to breathe life into an otherwise unvisited street. Her lovely boutique sells paintings and miniatures by Turkish artists, hand-painted ceramics, costume jewellery and calligraphy that make for beautiful Istanbul souvenirs.

192 **LEVAN**
Asmalı Mescit Mh.
Hazzopulo Pasajı 3-E
Beyoğlu ①
+90 212 243 60 16

This small boutique hidden away in the lively Hazzopulo arcade sells beautiful handcrafted jewellery from Anatolia. From a delicate necklace with rubies to a woven bracelet made from silver and silk, Levan's collections represent the various regions of Turkey through unique motifs and stories.

193 TURKISH MODERN

Firuzağa Mh.
Yeni Çarşı Cd. 27-A
Beyoğlu ①
+90 534 313 61 55
turkishmodern.com

Run by Istanbul native Şeyda Doğan Carter and her husband Alexander B. Carter, this gorgeous shop is all about keeping traditional Turkish design alive. Produced exclusively by skilled craftswomen and men, you'll find beautiful furniture, textiles and leatherware made with love. The shop also has a branch in San Francisco.

194 ATELIER REBUL

Harbiye Mh.
Teşvikiye Cd. 31
Şişli ③
+90 534 891 64 65
atelierrebul.com.tr

Established in 1895, the historic Rebul pharmacy was famous for its perfumes and personal care items preferred by Istanbul's bourgeoisie. Nowadays, Atelier Rebul continues to produce its famously fragrant *kolonya* (eau de cologne) in scents such as mandarin, lavender, jasmine or fig, as well as creams, lotions and shampoos.

195 BUTIK KATIA

Asmalı Mescit Mh.
Hazzopulo Pasajı 4-C
Beyoğlu ①
+90 212 249 46 05
butik-katia.business.site

Travel back to Istanbul in the 1930s when it was unimaginable to leave the house without a hat designed by milliner Eva. Her daughter Katia Kiracı continues her mother's handcrafted legacy of elegance to this day and Madame Katia's royal-style hats are custom-made and of high-quality materials imported from Europe.

The 5 best

VINYL RECORD STORES

196 **ANALOG KÜLTÜR**
Şahkulu Mh.
Seraskerci Çk. 4-A
Beyoğlu ①
+90 212 287 10 84
analogkultur.com

This hidden basement is a real treasure for music lovers and was opened by Kaan Düzarat, one of the city's most important DJs whose vast knowledge of Turkish music is pretty much unmatched. You'll find both Turkish and international secondhand and original records as well as vintage audio equipment.

197 **DEFORM MÜZIK**
Kuloğlu Mh.
Turnacıbaşı Cd. 45
Beyoğlu ①
+90 212 245 33 37

A record store for the truly passionate vinyl collectors out there, Deform stands out with its large collection of ethnic music, and house, disco and techno singles. You'll find an excellent archive of secondhand records of Turkish and international artists as well as demos, magazines, fanzines and cassettes.

198 LALE PLAK

Şahkulu Mh.
Galipdede Cd. 1
Beyoğlu ①
+90 212 293 77 39

Befittingly located on a street known for its musical instrument shops, Lale Plak has been around since the 1960s and is run by two brothers who love music. The collection, which is composed of new editions only, focusses heavily on jazz, but also includes classic, rock, blues and Turkish artists.

199 KONTRA RECORD STORE

Tomtom Mh.
Yeni Çarşı Cd. 60-A
Beyoğlu ①
+90 212 243 86 80
kontrarecords.com

Kontra Plak may be one of the newer additions to Istanbul's record store scene but it has still managed to become one of the best places for secondhand vinyl. Browse through the nicely organised A-Z racks where you'll come across various genres from jazz to hip-hop to electronic.

200 OPUS 3A

Pürtelaş Hasan Efendi Mh.
Cihangir Cd. 3-A
Beyoğlu ①
+90 212 251 84 05
opus3a.com

One of the bigger record stores in Istanbul, Opus 3a has more than one thousand records to its name and is another music collection well worth a browse. There's a heavy focus on jazz and classic music, but you'll also find music from the iconic Turkish musicians from the psychedelic 1970s era.

5 places for great
HOME DÉCOR

201 **HIÇ CONTEMPORARY CRAFTS**
Hacı Mimi Mh.
Lüleci Hendek Sk. 35
Beyoğlu ①
+90 212 251 99 73
hiccrafts.com

This shop, opened by interior designer Emel Güntaş, features one-of-a-kind home décor objects from passionate artisans and designers from all over Turkey and further east. The collection includes colourful Turkish coffeepots with wooden handles, hand-printed and illustrated silk scarves, ceramics with Islamic calligraphy and pillows with traditional Anatolian designs.

201 HIÇ CONTEMPORARY CRAFTS

202 **SPACE CACTUS**

Firuzağa Mh.
Faik Paşa Cd. 51-A
Beyoğlu ①
+90 535 825 73 31
spacecactus.info

Enter into a world of cacti and succulents that have been collected since the 1980s from Bodrum and the areas around it. A real paradise of green, this botanic boutique also sells ceramics, floral art and other design objects meant to add a natural touch to one's home.

203 **NESLIHAN ALGÜNERHAN**

İnönü Mh.
Elmadağ Cad. 1
Arifpaşa Apt. 12-D
Şişli ③
neslihan algunerhan.com

You'll only be able to see this Istanbul textile designer's collection of table cloths, runners and napkins, handcrafted through natural dye printing, by contacting her through Instagram and making an appointment. Neslihan's inspiration is nature, which is clearly reflected in her creations that bear the beauty of flora and fauna.

204 **HAM:M**

Teşvikiye Mh.
Akkavak Sk. 10-A
Şişli ③
+90 533 681 90 70
hamm.com.tr

Founded by architects Muhammet Taşlı and İdil Özbek in 2010, Ham:m is one of the best places in Istanbul to buy modern furniture handmade by local artisans. The Ham:m Nişantaşı shop also features home décor goods from local designers that go quite well with their Scandinavian design-inspired furniture.

205 **3 THINGS ON AN ISLAND**

Pelit Sk. 2-A
Burgazada ⑧

A tiny concept shop on the laidback and car-free Burgaz island with colourful handmade ceramics, decorative silk pillows, botanic-print clutches and natural beauty products. Make sure to ask about their monthly arts and crafts workshops.

5

BOOKSHOPS

for passionate bookworms

206 **MINOA BOOKSTORE**
Vişnezade Mh.
Süleyman Seba
Cd. 52-A
Beşiktaş ③
+90 212 236 94 52

A cafe and bookstore, Minoa is the perfect place to buy a book and then settle down with some coffee and start reading. You'll also be happy to know that Minoa's English language section features the latest releases from the world of fiction and non-fiction.

207 **ENVAI BEBEK**
Bebek Mh.
Cevdet Paşa Cd. 57-B
Beşiktaş ④
+90 212 265 29 91

Definitely stop by this charming little bookshop in the Bebek neighbourhood that carries a great selection of second-hand Turkish books (as well as some English titles). This is also the place to pick up a copy of *Cornucopia* magazine and to shop for souvenirs such as brightly coloured ceramics or postcards.

208 HOMER KITABEVI

Tomtom Mh.
Yeni Çarşı Cd. 52
Beyoğlu ①
+90 212 249 59 02
homerbooks.com

An independent bookstore that has been open since 1995, Homer is the source for works on Byzantine and Turkish history by local and international authors. Even though its archaeology and history books are in the forefront, the bookstore has also increased its scope in the areas of photography and philosophy as well as children's books.

209 DENIZLER KITABEVI

Tomtom Mh.
İstiklal Cd. 199-A
Beyoğlu ①
+90 212 249 88 93
denizler.org

With its winding wooden staircase in the background and a space filled with antique books and objects, Denizler Kitabevi is certainly one of Istanbul's most beautiful bookstores. Founded in 1993, Denizler carries an excellent selection of titles on maritime history as well as rare books and old maps.

210 ROBINSON CRUSOE 389

Asmalı Mescit Mh.
İstiklal Cd. 136, 1st Fl.
Beyoğlu ①
+90 212 293 69 68
rob389.com

Located inside the very modern SALT Beyoğlu art gallery, you'll want to spend hours inside this very quiet and serene bookshop that has an excellent selection of English titles. Browse classics and new releases as well as English editions of works by Turkish authors.

5 of the city's best
ANTIQUE SHOPS

211 **SOFA**
Şahkulu Mh.
Seraskerci Çk. 2
Beyoğlu ①
+90 212 520 28 50
kashifsofa.com

Established in 1976, SOFA is one of Istanbul's most important antique dealers and you'll know why as soon as you enter their shop filled with select paintings, mosaics, embroidery, calligraphy and much more. Also make sure to have a chat with the owner Kaşif who is an absolute delight and an endless source of information.

212 **A LA TURCA**
Çukurcuma Mh.
Faikpaşa Sk. 4
Beyoğlu ①
+90 532 314 36 81
alaturcahouse.com

Ring the doorbell and enter Erkal Aksoy's haven of beautiful antiques that perfectly decorate the rooms of a historic townhouse in Çukurcuma. Like a visual history lesson of the Ottoman era, every inch of A la Turca hides another beautiful object, whether it be carpets, pottery, antique globes or paintings.

213 SAH GALERI

Caferağa Mh.
Tellalzade Sk. 9-A
Kadiköy ⑦
+90 216 346 12 13

Tellalzade Street is the main artery of Kadıköy's lesser-known antiques quarter and this is where you'll find Sah Galeri, a shop that stands out from the rest. Run by the overtly charming Yenen couple, the antique toys, games and posters are especially notable, as well as framed illustrations by Ayşegül Yenen herself.

214 DADA KUZGUNCUK

Kuzguncuk Mh.
Perihan Abla Sk. 6
Üsküdar ⑤
+90 216 532 76 62
dadakuzguncuk.com

The owners of this lovely antique shop, in a historic and beautifully renovated Kuzguncuk apartment, showcase their rare finds according to regularly changing themes. All their treasures come from a large depot in Tuzla, which is constantly being updated with new discoveries. Most notable is their collection of antique toys..

215 HORHOR ANTIQUES BAZAAR

İskenderpaşa Mh.
Kırık Tulumba Sk. 13
Fatih ②

With its more than 200 shops filled with antiques that specialise in different eras and geographies, the Horhor Antiques Bazaar is definitely for serious antique hunters who want to spend a day perusing potential treasures. Don't hesitate to chat with the very knowledgeable shopkeepers who are always keen to share the facts.

212 **A LA TURCA**

5 great shops for

OTTOMAN / ANATOLIAN INSPIRED DESIGN

216 **ARMAGGAN**
Halaskargazi Mh.
Süleyman Nazif
Sk. 38
Şişli ③
+90 212 241 65 80
armaggan.com

A socially and environmentally conscious luxury brand, Armaggan represents the seamless confluence of contemporary design with the cultural heritage of Anatolian civilizations. Expertly handcrafted jewellery collections, objets d'art, leather goods and naturally dyed textiles are all inspired by ancient Anatolian and Ottoman motifs and exude a unique opulence.

217 **GÖNÜL PAKSOY**
Nişantaşı Mh.
Akkavak Sk.,
Demet Apt 4-A
Şişli ③
+90 212 236 02 09
gonulpaksoy.com

The work of fashion designer, artist and author Gönül Paksoy should really be hanging in a museum. Beautiful hand-dyed silks in earthy tones come together in Paksoy's unique style inspired by the garments worn by Sufi dervishes. Let's not forget the magnificent beads that complement every outfit (and on which Paksoy wrote a two-volume book).

218 URART

Nişantaşı Mh.
Abdi İpekçi Cd. 18-1
Şişli ③
+90 212 246 71 94
urart.com.tr

This high-end boutique is all about fascinatingly beautiful handcrafted jewellery inspired by the Anatolian civilizations and the Ottoman era. You'll find ornate golden rings with Anatolian motifs or delicate charm necklaces with precious stones as well as decorative objects from glass, silver, marble, brass and bronze.

219 TANER ALAKUŞ MINIATURE ATELIER

Dervişali Mh.
Kariye Türbe Sk. 20
Fatih ②
+90 212 635 43 51
taneralakus.com

Hidden away on a side street by the Chora Church, Taner Alakuş's shop and atelier is all about the beautiful art of Ottoman miniature painting. Browse the very talented artist's stunningly minute and colourful illustrations of an Istanbul where sultans still ruled and take one home with you as a unique memento.

220 ELLER

Tomtom Mh.
Postacılar Sk. 4-A
Beyoğlu ①
+90 212 249 23 64
ellerartgallery.wordpress.com is

With opera music playing in the background, talented craftsman Nurhan Acun works on another beautiful piece of handmade jewellery inspired by the motifs of ancient Anatolian civilizations in this hidden atelier and shop. Don't hesitate to try things on, or to ask for something custom-made, Acun will love to converse with you about his craft.

The 5 shops with unique
LOCAL HANDMADE DESIGN

221 HAYDANHUYA

Müeyyetzade Mh.
Lüleci Hendek Cd. 62
Beyoğlu ①
haydanhuya.com

Gökhan Eryaman has been quietly creating magnificent objects from natural wood in his atelier that's hidden away on a side street where only the informed know to wander. An artisan with a deep passion for slow-living and true handcraftsmanship, Eryaman's wooden bags, wallets, brushes, and tableware are custom-made by him personally and with love.

222 MAITOINEN.

Feneryolu Mh.
Gazi Muhtarpaşa
Sk. 37-C
Kadıköy ⑦

Inspired by Scandinavian minimalism, the Finnish word for 'milky,' and her time working at Monet's Garden in Giverny, Zehra's unique ceramic tableware collections express how subtle touches of colour create endearingly subdued beauty.

223 KULAK CERAMIC

Muradiye Mh.
Muradiye Bayırı
Sk. 39
Şişli ③
+90 212 531 3748
kulakceramic.com

It's the small human imperfections that make the ceramics of Zeynep Saraçoğlu and Pınar Philliskirk so beautiful and unique. Every glazed or unglazed cup, bowl, dish or plate in earthy tones has been lovingly created by hand adding a genuinely warm and Istanbul-made touch to any home.

224 ÇUVAL

Arnavutköy Mh.
Beyazgül Cd. 53
Beşiktaş ④
+90 532 257 92 68
shop.cuvalist.com

A contemporary accessories brand that is all about supporting and promoting local craftsmanship, Çuval's bags are not only 100% Turkish-made but also downright gorgeous. Established in 2012 by Ayşe Özgüneş, Çuval features such goodies as suede drawstring buckets, leather belt-bags and beach bags from vegetable-tanned leather.

225 BAGO

Arnavutköy Mh.
Arnavutköy Bebek Cd. 15
Kristal Apt. K:1 D:1
Beşiktaş ④
+90 533 315 97 78
bagohandicrafts.com

With a name that translates to 'spirit of forest,' in Far Eastern mythology, Bago is an accessories label that is thoroughly exotic. Gorgeous clutches and bags made from 100% natural materials such as palm or banana tree leaves, pineapple leaves, and mother-of-pearl actively support craftmanship and artisans in the Philippines, Mexico, Brazil and Turkey. Aiming to support and empower artisan women, the brand, founded by İpek Kocatepe, only uses organic and non-chemical dyes and heightens its designs with genuine gemstones such as agate, quartz, lapis, jade and onyx.

The 5 best places for

SECONDHAND BOOKS

226 **TURKUAZ SAHAF**
Kuloğlu Mh.
Gazeteci Erol Dernek Sk. 5, Erman Han
3rd Fl., Apt. 7
Beyoğlu ①
+90 212 245 45 88
sahaf-turkuaz.com

A *sahaf* in Turkish may be a secondhand bookseller but Turkuaz Sahaf is more akin to a museum of books loved by bookworms, book collectors and academicians alike. Titles, which have warranted their own exhibitions, traverse such areas as history, literature, philosophy and art in languages such as German, Ottoman, Armenian, Greek and Hebrew.

227 **SAHAF MÜTEFERRIKA**
Caferağa Mh.
Mühürdar Cd. 70-23
Kadıköy ⑦
+90 216 336 47 34

One of Kadıköy's best bookshops is right in its busy market but has somehow remained a local secret. Run by Lütfi Seymen, Müteferrika has a fantastic collection of rare books as well as antique postcards, magazines, Ottoman manuscripts and photographs.

228 KITAP RAFI SAHAF

Caferağa Mh.
Sarraf Ali Sk. 17-A
Kadıköy ⑦
+90 532 736 21 45
kitaprafisahaf.com

A favourite bookshop amongst history enthusiasts who have a soft spot for Ottoman and Byzantine history or book collectors who want to browse through thousands of beautiful titles, Kitap Rafı is another one of Kadıköy's intellectual secrets. Don't hesitate to chat with the knowledgeable owner Özgür Harman if you can't find what you're looking for.

229 SAHAFLAR ÇARŞISI / BOOK BAZAAR

Beyazıt Mh.
Çadırcılar Cd.
Fatih ②

The Sahaflar Çarşısı opened in 1954, but the site itself goes back to the Byzantine and Ottoman eras when it was used as a book market and trading centre. Nowadays, the book bazaar mostly sells secondhand schoolbooks, but if you do a little digging, you'll be rewarded with historic maps, texts and other rare finds.

230 ASLIHAN PASAJI BOOK BAZAAR

Hüseyinağa Mh.
Meşrutiyet Cd. 10
Beyoğlu ①

This hidden passage is full of secondhand booksellers and you'll want to spend hours foraging through all the potential treasures. Among the seemingly endless stacks and racks of books in various languages you'll also find vintage film posters, postcards, maps and magazines.

5 shops for amazing

TURKISH JEWELLERY

231 DER-LIEBLING

Şahkulu Mh.
Serdar-ı Ekrem
Cd. 44-A
Beyoğlu ①
+90 535 035 46 45
der-liebling.com

After working as an apprentice for master jewellery artisan Eren Özler in the Grand Bazaar for two years, Banu Kent went on to establish her own jewellery brand, Der-Liebling. Her unique ethnic-style collections are a manifestation of her fine-tuned talent as well as inspirations gathered from her many travels to countries like India. Visits by appointment only.

232 MAYIS

Tomtom Mh.
İstiklal Cd. 199
Beyoğlu ①
+90 212 293 75 43

Not a lot of people stop to gander inside this treasure of a shop, which is more like a museum of rare and beautiful handcrafted silver rings, necklaces and earrings that are becoming harder to find due to the popularity of the cheap and mass-produced. Mayıs also has a lovely collection of hand-painted ceramics.

233 ALEF

Tesvikiye Mh.
Haci Emin Efendi Sk. 4-A
Şişli ③
+90 212 241 35 58
alef.com.tr

Living in a city that is a constant source of inspiration, jewellery designer Yeşim Yüksek's collections blend various aesthetics, from Art Deco to the Middle Ages to the contemporary. Materials such as blue topaz, quartz, onyx and aquamarine appear frequently in minimal designs that speak boldly.

234 YUKA

Vişnezade Mh.
Maçka Meydanı Sk. 18-A
Beşiktaş ③
+90 212 259 10 99
yukabyguliz.com

Güliz Mustafaoğlu's small jewellery boutique and atelier is hidden away on a quiet residential street in Beşiktaş. Inside you'll find lovingly handmade and beautifully modern geometric necklaces and rings with colourful stones or large gold earrings in the shape of fine leaves.

235 AIDA BERGSEN

Teşvikiye Mh.
Bostan Sk. 11/2
Şişli ③
aidabergsen.com

The wearable sculptures of jewellery designer Aida Bergsen, inspired by mythology as well as organic forms, are crafted in wax before they are transformed into utterly unique jewels. Think of bejewelled snake-shaped rings, thick necklaces bedecked in blooming flowers or headpieces with ornate wings.

5 *of the best spots to buy* CARPETS

236 **VEZIRHAN**
Mollafenari Mh.
Gazi Sinan Paşa Sk. 1
Fatih ②
+90 212 519 55 10
vezirhancarpet.com

Located inside a building that dates back to 1635, when it was used as a staff house for the Ottoman viziers and later as a caravanserai, nowadays Vezirhan is a carpet paradise. All carpets are handmade from select materials and dyes and woven on handlooms at the store's production facility in Van and nearby villages.

237 **GÜNEŞ ÖZTARAKÇI**
Harbiye Mh.
Mim Kemal Öke
Cd. 5
Şişli ③
+90 212 225 19 54

A real local secret when it comes to excellent carpet shopping, Güneş Öztarakçı was the first woman to open a carpet showroom in Turkey. You'll find antique Turkish carpets of very high quality in her shop and will quickly notice that Öztarakçı approaches her carefully selected wares as works of art with cultural significance.

238 HAZAL KİLİM

Ortaköy Mh.
Mecidiye Köprüsü
Sk. 9
Beşiktaş ③
+90 212 261 72 33
hazalkilim.com

You'll find this family-run business inside a lovely historic apartment in the Ortaköy neighbourhood just a few steps away from the Bosphorus. Engin and Ahmet Demirkol and their daughter Hazal specialise in beautiful vintage and antique Anatolian rugs as well as custom-made carpet pillows.

239 ETHNICON AND DHOKU

AT: GRAND BAZAAR
Takkeciler Sk. 58-60
Fatih ②
+90 212 527 68 41
dhoku.com
ethnicon.com

Ethnicon and Dhoku are both owned by Memet Güreli who comes from three generations of Turkish rug experts. Located right across each other, Ethnicon and Dhoku blend Turkish antique and ethnic aesthetic in order to create contemporary Turkish carpets, all of which are handwoven on looms around Anatolia.

240 NAKKAŞ

Sultanahmet Mh.
Nakilbent Sk. 6
Fatih ②
+90 212 516 52 22
nakkasrug.com

There's a lot to take in at Nakkaş including more than 20.000 beautiful handwoven carpets from regions all over Turkey as well as jewellery, ceramics and antiques. If that didn't suffice, there's also a restored 6th-century cistern downstairs that's used as an art gallery.

5 shops to buy everything for an

@HOME TURKISH BATH

241 **HOMEMADE AROMATHERAPY**
Kuzguncuk Mh.
Üryanizade Sk. 5
Üsküdar ⑤
+90 216 310 54 07
homemade aromaterapi.com

Produced and sold in the Homemade Aromatherapy shop in Kuzguncuk, this beautiful boutique aims to spread its love for organic and cold-pressed essential herbal oils. Apart from the fragrant oils, you'll also be tempted to envelop yourself in lavender water, goat's milk soap, rose and geranium natural deodorant or coconut oil (just to name a few).

242 **SAFIYE SABUN**
Cumhuriyet Mh.
Kazım Orbay Cd. 40
Şişli ③
+90 212 599 20 46
safiye.com.tr

Celebrating Anatolia's traditional art of soap-making, Safiye is a modern boutique that sells handmade and 100% organic soaps. The enticing smells of lavender, cinnamon, apricot-laurel, and coffee-cocoa soaps are derived purely from essential oils without any additives.

243 **ABDULLA NATURAL PRODUCTS**
Molla Fenari Mh.
Alibaba Türbe Sk. 15
Fatih ②
+90 212 526 30 70
abdulla.com

At Abdulla you'll find everything you need for a Turkish bath including hamam bowls, washing cloths, *takunya* (traditional wooden sandals), and *peştamal* towels, all from local and organic producers. Bulk buy their natural handmade oil soaps that come in many different fragrances.

244 KILIÇ ALI PAŞA HAMAM SHOP
Kemankeş Mh.
Hamam Sk. 1
Beyoğlu ①
+90 212 393 80 10
kilicalipasa hamami.com

You'll be happy to know that one of Istanbul's best hamams also has its own shop where it sells all the products used during the Turkish bath sessions inside. You'll find everything from traditional hamam bowls and wooden *takunya* sandals to colourful *peştamal* towels and bathrobes as well as natural fabric clothing and souvenirs.

245 JENNIFER'S HAMAM
Sultanahmet Mh.
Arasta Bazaar 135
Fatih ②
+90 212 516 30 22
jennifershamam.com

This shop is named after its Canadian owner Jennifer Gaudet who supports and works with some of the last families in Turkey who continue the country's weaving tradition on shuttled looms. Fluffy bath towels and *peştamals*, scarves, bed and home textiles are all made from organically sourced cotton and linen.

241 HOMEMADE AROMATHERAPY

YILDIZ HAMIDIYE MOSQUE

60 BUILDINGS TO ADMIRE

5 stunning works by Italian architect
RAIMONDO D'ARONCO

246 **VLORA HAN**
Hobyar Mh.
Büyük Postane
Cd. 14-B
Fatih ②

Chief palace architect to Abdülhamid II, Italian innovator Raimondo D'Aronco helped the sultan realise his ideal of a modern Ottoman identity. Underneath a layer of dilapidation, the art nouveau wonder that is the Vlora Han (from the early 1900s) continues to reveal its magnificent details to those who take a moment to appreciate it.

247 **SHEIKH ZAFIR MAUSOLEUM**
Cihannüma Mh.
Mehmet ali Bey Sk.
Beşiktaş ③

Part of the Ertuğrul Tekke mosque complex, this ornate mausoleum was built by D'Aronco in 1905 for Abdülhamid II's spiritual confidant, Libyan Sufi Sheikh Zafir al-Madani. Combining the Ottoman and art nouveau styles, the beautiful structure's most notable detail is the reinterpreted *muqarna* (ornamented vaulting).

248 **BOTTER APARTMENT**

Şahkulu Mh.
İstiklal Cd. 235
Beyoğlu ①

Thousands of people walk by this art nouveau apartment with stone roses and embellished wrought iron balconies on a daily basis without taking a second glance. Built by D'Aronco in the early 1900s, the structure served as the workshop and residence of Jean Botter, Abdülhamid II's couturier.

249 **YILDIZ PORSELEN FACTORY AND MUSEUM**

AT: YILDIZ KORUSU
Yıldız Mh.
Yıldız Cd. 62
Beşiktaş ③

Sultan Abdülhamid II established the imperial porcelain factory around 1890 due to a demand for European-style ceramics, and after an earthquake damaged the original structure, the reconstruction was led by D'Aronco. Nowadays, the factory continues to produce the beautiful Yıldız Porselen wares sold in the museum and shop next door.

250 **SUMMER RESIDENCE OF THE ITALIAN AMBASSADOR**

Tarabya Mh.
Haydar Aliyev Cd. 146
Sarıyer ⑥

This stunning wooden Bosphorus mansion has sadly fallen into a state of disrepair and can only be admired from afar, especially whilst riding the Eminönü-Rumeli Kavağı Bosphorus ferry line. Built in Palladian style by D'Aronco in 1905, the mansion served as the summer residence of the Italian ambassador.

Levantine architect
ALEXANDER VALLAURY's
5 everlasting structures

251 PERA PALACE

Evliya Çelebi Mh.
Meşrutiyet Cd. 52
Beyoğlu ①
+90 212 377 40 00
perapalace.com

Born in Istanbul to an Italian father and educated in Paris, architect Alexander Vallaury's most famous work is the neoclassical, art nouveau and oriental-style Pera Palace. Built in 1892, Pera was the only Istanbul hotel that had hot water and electricity, serving passengers of the Orient Express.

252 ISTANBUL HIGH SCHOOL

Hobyar Mh.
Türk Ocağı Cd. 4
Fatih ②
+90 212 514 15 70

Only viewable from the outside, Vallaury's Ottoman Public Debt Administration building was opened in 1897, but has been used as the Istanbul High School (one of Turkey's oldest and most eminent high schools) since 1933. The remarkable structure abides to the aesthetic of the First National Architectural Movement, or Turkish neoclassical architecture.

253 ISTANBUL ARCHAEOLOGY MUSEUM

Cankurtaran Mh.
Alemdar Cd.
Fatih ②
+90 212 520 77 40
istanbularkeoloji.gov.tr

Construction of the museum's main building was initiated by Ottoman painter and archaeologist Osman Hamdi Bey in 1881 with Vallaury as the architect. Inspired by the Alexander Sarcophagus (which is on display inside), the imposing marble-columned structure is a masterpiece of neo-Greek architecture.

254 IMPERIAL COLLEGE OF MEDICINE

AT: MARMARA UNIVERSITY FACULTY OF LAW
Selimiye Mh.
Tıbbiye Cd. 38
Üsküdar ⑤
+90 216 349 84 00

As professor and founder of the in 1882-established Istanbul École des Beaux-Arts' architecture department (now Mimar Sinan University), it seems only natural for Vallaury to have worked with D'Aronco to design the Imperial College of Medicine. Only viewable from the outside, the Haydarpaşa Campus of Marmara University (as it's called today) is a truly fascinating structure of Turkish neoclassical architecture.

255 HIDAYET MOSQUE

Hobyar Mh.
Yalı Köşkü Cd. 8
Fatih ②

Reconstructed in 1887, the Hidayet Mosque is one of Vallaury's lesser known works, quietly hiding away behind the busy streets of Eminönü. With decorative pointed-frame windows added to a mostly simple façade, Hidayet exemplifies clearly how Vallaury's classicist fundamentals adopted contrasting Islamic-Ottoman elements.

5 beautiful buildings by Italian architect GIULIO MONGERI

256 **BULGUR PALACE**
Aksaray Mh.
Kargı Çk. 5
Fatih ②

The prominent Levantine-Italian architect Giulio Mongeri worked on this splendid brick palace in 1912 for Mehmet Habib Bey who made a fortune selling *bulgur* (cracked wheat), hence the name.
A fantastic example of the First National Architectural Movement, the palace's giant tower is especially imposing.

257 **CHURCH OF SAINT ANTOINE**
Tomtom Mh.
İstiklal Cd. 171
Beyoğlu ①
+90 212 244 09 35
sentantuan.com

Hiding in plain sight, the largest Roman Catholic Church in Istanbul is a beautiful vision of red brick and stone with vaulted ceilings in sky-blue. Built in 1906 by Giulio Mongeri and Edoardo de Nani, the Gothic-style church holds mass in different languages throughout the week.

258 **MAÇKA PALACE**
Teşvikiye Mh.
Bronz Sk. 4
Şişli ③
+90 212 315 12 34
hyatt.com

Built in 1922 by Mongeri, this grandiose art deco structure was home to the Italian diplomats of the time. Nowadays, you'll have to book a room at the very chic Park Hyatt Istanbul in order to inspect the interior, or visit the boutiques on street level including Emporio Armani and Gucci.

259 BOZLU HOLDING BUILDING

19 Mayıs Mh.
Dr. Şevket Bey Sk. 5
Şişli ③
+90 212 233 72 33
bozluartproject.com

A fantastic structure of the First National Architectural Movement hidden in the midst of Şişli's high-rise offices and hotels, this Mongeri beauty stands out with its large domed tower and shining blue tiled panels. Built in 1925 and since fully restored, the former headquarters of Bozlu Holding now serves as the Bozlu Art Project art gallery.

260 KARAKÖY PALACE

Kemankeş Mh.
Havyar Haniçi Sk.
Beyoğlu ①

Once the Ottoman Empire's grand banking district, nowadays the Karaköy area is a jumble of historic structures and newer constructions. Built in 1920, the beautiful Karaköy Palas is a testament to the past having once housed the Banco di Roma and Banca Commerciale Italiana.

257 CHURCH OF SAINT ANTOINE

5 *iconic structures designed by the*

OTTOMAN ARMENIAN BALYAN FAMILY

261 **BEYLERBEYI PALACE**
Beylerbeyi Mh.
Abdullah Ağa Cd.
Üsküdar ⑤
+90 216 321 93 20
millisaraylar.gov.tr

Nine members of the renowned Ottoman-Armenian Balyan family served as court architects for the Ottoman sultans for five generations. The opulent white marble, neo-baroque Beylerbeyi Palace, once used to entertain foreign dignitaries, is just one example of the Balyan's magnificent style with refined details such as Bohemian crystal chandeliers and elaborate frescoes.

262 **YILDIZ HAMIDIYE MOSQUE**
Cihannüma Mh.
Serencebey Ykş. 63
Beşiktaş ③

Even though the Yıldız Palace is no longer accessible to visitors, the nearby gates of the Yıldız Hamidiye Mosque are always open. Built between 1884 and 1886 by Sarkis Balyan, the beautiful mosque is a confluence of Moorish, neo-Gothic and European Orientalism architectural styles. Most notable is the deep blue dome with sparkling golden stars.

263 ÜÇ HORAN CHURCH

Hüseyinağa Mh.
Sahne Sk. 24-1
Beyoğlu ①
+90 212 244 13 82

Hidden away in a courtyard by the bustling Galatasaray fish market, the 19th-century Üç Horan (Three Altars) Church is quite the surprise with its large marble exterior. Past its large wooden doors is a beautiful altar with ornate chandeliers and Corinthian columns.

264 DOLMABAHÇE PALACE

Vişnezade Mh.
Dolmabahçe Cd.
Beşiktaş ③
+90 212 236 90 00
millisaraylar.gov.tr

When Sultan Abdül Mecit I decided to move the imperial court from Topkapı to the Bosphorus, the overtly lavish Dolmabahçe Palace in Ottoman-European style was designed and completed by Nikoğos and Garabed Balyan in 1854. The designer of the Paris Opera was also brought in to design the palace's stunning interior.

265 ADILE SULTAN PALACE

Kandilli Mh.
Vaniköy Cd. 12
Üsküdar ④
+90 216 332 23 33
adilesultan.org

This Sarkis Balyan-designed Bosphorus palace was the former residence of princess Adile Sultan. A firm believer in education, the princess' home became a girl's school in 1899, and after a damaging fire, it was restored by the businessman and philanthropist Sakıp Sabancı in 1986 and is now used for events.

5 *important works by*
MIMAR SINAN

266 **BÜYÜKÇEKMECE BRIDGE**
Mimarsinan Mh.
Mimar Sinan Kavşağı
Büyükçekmece ⑨

Considered *the* greatest Ottoman architect, Mimar Sinan (Architect Sinan) held the title of State Architect for a decade, beginning under the reign of Sultan Süleyman. Built between 1566 and 1567 and composed of four connected arch bridges on artificial islands, the Büyükçekmece Bridge is one of Sinan's lesser-known but equally magnificent works.

266 BÜYÜKÇEKMECE BRIDGE

267 **MIHRIMAH SULTAN MOSQUE**

Karagümrük Mh.
Hacı Muhiddin Cami Sk.
Fatih ②

Commissioned by Sultan Süleyman for his favourite daughter princess Mihrimah, this imperial mosque complex was built by Sinan in the 1560s. There's another Mihrimah Sultan Mosque in Üsküdar, and according to legend the sun sets at the Edirnekapı mosque while the moon rises from the Üsküdar mosque annually on March 21 (the princess's birthday).

268 **ŞEHZADE MEHMET MOSQUE**

Kalenderhane Mh.
Şehzadebaşı Cd. 44
Fatih ②

Commissioned by Süleyman the Magnificent to honour the memory of his son Mehmet who died of smallpox at the age of 22, Şehzade Mehmet is Sinan's first major sultanic mosque. Built between 1544 and 1555, the octagonal mausoleum of Mehmet and the mosque's beautiful minarets are worthy of admiration.

269 **RÜŞTEM PAŞA MOSQUE**

Rüştem Paşa Mh.
Hasırcılar Cd. 62
Fatih ②

Hidden away in the backstreets near Eminönü Square, Sinan built this beautiful structure for Rüştem Paşa, Grand Vizier to Süleyman the Magnificent in 1563. Known fondly as a smaller version of the Blue Mosque without the crowds, the mosque is notable for its incredible Iznik tile decoration.

270 **SOKULLU MEHMET PAŞA MOSQUE**

Küçük Ayasofya Mh.
Şht. Mehmet Paşa Sk. 15
Fatih ②

Designed in 1571 for Sokullu Mehmet Paşa's wife, actual pieces of the Ka'aba in Mecca were used in the construction of this mosque's mihrab and mimber. The beautiful Iznik tiles and stained-glass windows inside are also quite exceptional.

The 5 most impressive works of MODERNIST ARCHITECTURE

271 FLORYA ATATÜRK MARINE MANSION

Basınköy Mh.
Çekmece İstanbul Cd. 23
Bakırköy ⑨
+90 212 426 51 51

Far away from urban pandemonium, Atatürk's former summer home is a Bauhaus dream that seems to hover above the sea. Built in 1935 by the Turkish architect Seyfi Erkan (who studied in Berlin and worked alongside Hans Poelzig), the museum looks out over the water from every room decked out in original Bauhaus furniture.

272 HILTON ISTANBUL BOSPHORUS

Harbiye Mh.
Cumhuriyet Cd. 50
Şişli ③
+90 212 315 60 00
hilton.com

The Istanbul Hilton Hotel was built by the prominent American firm Skidmore, Owings & Merrill with Sedad Hakkı Eldem (a pioneer in Turkish nationalised modern architecture) acting as advisor. A confluence of modern architecture and Ottoman/Turkish touches, the hotel's grand opening in 1955 was attended by a slew of American celebrities.

271 FLORYA ATATÜRK MARINE MANSION

273 ISTANBUL METROPOLITAN MUNICIPALITY

Kemal Paşa Mh.
Temmuz Şehitleri Cd. 15
Fatih ②
+90 212 455 13 00

An underappreciated work of modernist architecture, the Istanbul Metropolitan Municipality was built by architect Nevzat Erol between 1953 and 1960. A fantastic concrete behemoth with almost futuristic parabolic curvilinear covers in light blue on the roof, the structure represents the era's clear transition in architecture due to international influences.

274 İSTANBUL MANIFATURACILAR ÇARŞISI

Zeyrek Mh.
Atatürk Blv.
Fatih ②
+90 212 526 52 83
imc.org.tr

İMÇ (Istanbul Draper's Bazaar) built by architects Metin Hepgüler, Sami Sisa and Doğan Tekeli, opened in 1967 and is one of Istanbul's prime modernist structures. From its unobtrusive horizontal construction to the beautiful spiral staircases, İMÇ also awakens pure admiration with nine art panels as well as sculptures from important names in Turkish contemporary art.

275 SSK ZEYREK TESISLERI

Cibali Mh.
Haşim İşcan Gç. 21
Fatih ②
+90 212 534 69 30

Right across İMÇ you'll find the equally underappreciated modernist structure that is the SSK (Social Security Administration) Building completed by architect Sedad Hakkı Eldem between 1962 and 1964. A confluence of modernist lines and Turkish/Ottoman details make for a downright spectacular work.

5 underappreciated OTTOMAN ERA STRUCTURES

276 HAYDARPAŞA RAILWAY STATION
Rasimpaşa Mh.
Kadıköy ⑦
+90 216 348 80 20

Only viewable from the Kadıköy-bound ferries (due to the construction of a new rail line), the Haydarpaşa Railway Station is awash in nostalgia and was designed by architects Otto Ritter and Helmuth Conu in 1909. The neoclassical structure will always stand out with its fine embellished exterior of German and Italian stone masonry.

277 ISTANBUL GRAND POST OFFICE
Hobyar Mh.
Büyük Postane Cd. 9
Fatih ②

Built by Vedat Tek, one of the First Turkish National Architectural Movement's leaders, Istanbul's Grand Post Office is a stunning convergence of the neoclassical and Ottoman styles. Completed in 1909, the structure continues to serve as a post office where daily errands surely serve as an excuse to inspect the beautiful interior.

278 NUSRETIYE MOSQUE
Kılıçali Paşa Mh.
Meclis-i Mebusan Cd.
Beyoğlu ①

Often overlooked, the Nusretiye Cami is an excellent example of the mix between Ottoman and baroque styles. It's also no surprise that the mosque was built by Krikor Balyan, the name behind the equally ornate Beylerbeyi Palace.

279 4TH VAKIF HAN

Hobyar Mh.
Hamidiye Cd. 16
Fatih ②

Now serving as the Legacy Ottoman Hotel, the beautiful 4th Vakıf Han was originally designed in 1911 by architect Kemalettin Bey to serve as office blocks. A towering work of the First National Architectural Movement, the new hotel's design sadly doesn't do the grand historic exterior any justice.

280 KULELI MILITARY HIGH SCHOOL

Kuleli Mh.
Kuleli Cd. 56
Üsküdar ④

Take a stroll by the Bosphorus in Çengelköy to really take in this sprawling structure with its unmistakable towers. Designed by Garabet Balyan in 1843, the Kuleli Military High School was founded by Ottoman Sultan Abdülmecid I in 1845 and continues to serve as a military school.

280 KULELI MILITARY HIGH SCHOOL

5 hidden architectural
GEMS IN BÜYÜKADA

281 **CON PAŞA MANSION**
Büyükada-Nizam Mh.
Nizam Cd. 70
Adalar ⑧

This beautiful mansion with equally beautiful sculptures in its garden was built by the architect Achileus Policis for Lesbos-native Con Paşa (whose real name was Trasivolos Yannaros) in 1880. Unbeknownst to many visitors who stroll by this mansion daily, Con Paşa was in fact the Ottoman official who established regular ferry service to Istanbul's islands.

282 **MIZZI MANSION**
Büyükada-Nizam Mh.
Nizam Cd. 17
Adalar ⑧

Designed by Raimondo D'Aronco in 1894, the island's Red Palace is an astonishing fantasy of red pressed brick with a soaring corner tower. This was the former home of Dr. Lewis Mizzi, a Maltese Levantine lawyer who also owned the Levant Herald and Eastern Express newspapers.

285 TROTSKY HOUSE

283 ÇANKAYA 57

Büyükada-Nizam Mh.
Çankaya Cd. 57
Adalar ⑧

This beautiful twin mansion in white was built by an Armenian tradesman in 1907 for his two daughters and according to rumour Leon Trotsky also stayed here briefly during his exile. However, the house is more famous for having been used for the 2006-2008 Turkish TV show, *Hatırla Sevgili.*

284 PRINKIPO GREEK ORTHODOX ORPHANAGE

Büyükada-Maden Mh.
Adalar ⑧

Considered Europe's largest wooden building, the former Prinkipo Palace was constructed by Alexandre Vallaury in 1899 as a luxury hotel and casino but was sold in 1903 and donated to the Ecumenical Patriarchate of Constantinople who turned it into an orphanage. Forcefully closed in 1964, the structure is sadly in a state of disrepair.

285 TROTSKY HOUSE

Büyükada-Nizam Mh.
Hamlacı Sk. 6
Adalar ⑧

This beautiful yet crumbling mansion ensconced in the wild abandon of its garden was once the home of exiled revolutionary Leon Trotsky for four years in 1929. It was here that Trotsky looked out over the sea and wrote his autobiography and *History of the Russian Revolution.*

The 5 most beautiful WATERFRONT MANSIONS

286 **ZEKI PAŞA MANSION**
Rumeli Hisarı Mh.
Balta Limanı Hisar
Cd. 16
Sarıyer ⑥

With the giant Fatih Sultan Mehmet Bridge suspended above it, the Zeki Paşa Yalısı is a magnificent 19th-century baroque palace with a polygonal stone façade and arched windows. Built by Alexandre Vallaury, the Ottoman field marshal Müşir Zeki Paşa sadly only slept in one of his 19 bedrooms for a single night before being exiled.

287 **FAIK AND BEKIR MANSION**
Yeniköy Mh.
Daire Sk.
Sarıyer ⑥

This *yalı* (waterfront mansion) was designed by architect Raimondo D'Aronco between 1890 and 1895 abiding to an art nouveau aesthetic with plenty of ornamentation present on its shining white double façade. The home was originally built for Sara Sultan's two daughters but was later sold to Faik Kurtoğlu and Bekir Sıtkı Oyal and befittingly renamed.

286 **ZEKI PAŞA MANSION**

288 KONT OSTROROG MANSION

Kandilli Mh.
Göksu Cd. 19
Üsküdar ④

This beautiful *yalı* seems to have taken its colour from the famous red clay of Avanos, blending in harmoniously with the evergreen trees and the glistening Bosphorus. The 19th-century mansion belonged to Count Ostrorog, a former consultant in Islamic Law for the Ottoman Empire.

289 SADULLAH PAŞA MANSION

Çengelköy Mh.
Kaptanı Derya Seyit Ali Paşa Sk. 11
Üsküdar ④

Built toward the end of the 18th century, the Sadullah Paşa Yalısı is one of the oldest Bosphorus mansions. Intricate plaster moulding as well as painted decorations in Ottoman and baroque tradition (which were discovered during renovations in 1947) make this structure even more precious.

290 AHMET AFIF PAŞA MANSION

Yeniköy Mh.
Köybaşı Cd. 183
Sarıyer ⑥

This beautiful towering five-storey mansion with glorious fig-shaped turrets was commissioned to architect Alexandre Vallaury by Ahmet Afif Paşa and built between 1900 and 1910. The home's most famous guest was Agatha Christie who stayed here in 1933 whilst writing her famous book *Murder on the Orient Express.*

5
LIBRARIES
to fall in love with

291 **ATATÜRK LIBRARY**
Gümüşsuyu Mh.
Miralay Şefikbey
Sk. 6
Beyoğlu ①
+90 212 249 09 45
ataturkkitapligi.
ibb.gov.tr

With its hexagonal towers that seem to hover above their concrete base, the Atatürk Library is another fantastic modernist structure that was designed by the renowned Turkish architect Sedad Hakkı Eldem in 1973 during the 50th anniversary of the Turkish Republic. The library has more than 500.000 books and beautiful unobstructed views over the Bosphorus.

292 **AHMET HAMDI TANPINAR LITERATURE MUSEUM LIBRARY**
Alemdar Mh.
Alemdar Cd.
Fatih ②
+90 212 520 20 81
ahtemkutuphane.
gov.tr

Named after Ahmed Hamdi Tanpınar (one of the most important representatives of literary modernism in Turkey) this literary museum and library is dedicated to the rich history of Turkish literature with about 9000 books. The library itself is inside the beautiful 19th-century Procession Kiosk inside the Topkapı Palace's Gülhane Park.

293 ISTANBUL LIBRARY

Sultan Ahmet Mh.
Soğuk Çeşme Sk. 36
Fatih ②
+90 212 512 57 30

Inside a beautiful old Ottoman *konak* (wooden house), the Istanbul Kitaplığı offers a very comprehensive journey through Istanbul's history as told through books, monographs, European travellers' journals and memoirs, photographs, maps and engravings. Hidden between Hagia Sophia and Topkapı Palace, you can easily spend whole afternoons immersing yourself in Istanbul's fascinating past.

294 KADIKÖY MUNICIPALITY HISTORY LITERATURE AND ART LIBRARY

Caferağa Mh.
Rıhtım Cd. 2/3
Kadıköy ⑦
+90 216 337 86 54-55

A 30.000-book collection is open to the public in this beautiful 19th-century building designed by Armenian architect Yervant Terziyan. Try to grab a seat by the window where you'll be greeted by a view of the iconic Istanbul ferries gliding by undisturbed.

295 VITALI HAKKO CREATIVE INDUSTRIES LIBRARY

Altunizade Mh.
Kuşbakışı Sk. 35
Üsküdar ⑤
+90 216 554 07 00

The renowned Turkish fashion brand Vakko's stunning concrete-clad-in-glass headquarter was designed by New York based REX architects in 2006. Inside, you'll find Vakko's beautiful library full of equally beautiful books about fashion, architecture, photography and art, watched over lovingly by the very knowledgeable librarian (and author) Begüm Başoğlu. Visits by appointment only.

The 5 most

UNCONVENTIONAL MOSQUES

296 SANCAKLAR MOSQUE

Karağaç Mh.
Sırtköy Çiftliği
Mevkii G 84 Bulvarı
Büyükçekmece ⑨

Built by Emre Arolat Architects in 2012, the Sancaklar Cami (Mosque) is a truly staggering construction that could best be described as a mosque deconstructed. On the outskirts of Istanbul, Sancaklar's cave-like prayer room is illuminated by natural light but also hidden underneath a canopy where man-made and natural are at constant play.

297 ŞAKIRIN MOSQUE

Barbaros Mh.
Nuhkuyusu Cd. 2
Üsküdar ⑤

The only mosque to have ever been designed by a woman, Şakirin's interior is a modern ode to faith created by the talented designer Zeynep Fadıllıoğlu. From the turquoise mihrab to the bronze chandelier with dangling blown-glass in the shape of water drops, Şakirin is a truly outstanding visual achievement.

296 **SANCAKLAR CAMI**

298 PERTEVNIYAL VALIDE SULTAN MOSQUE

İskenderpaşa Mh.
Atatürk Blv. 3
Fatih ②

Almost inundated by the bustling traffic of the Aksaray junction, the Pertevniyal Valide Sultan Cami is often overlooked. Built by Sarkis and Agop Balyan between 1869 and 1871, the mosque deviated from the classic design and instead flourished in neo-Gothic details including a façade of minute embellishment.

299 ARAP MOSQUE

Arap Cami Mh.
Hoca Hanım Sk. 8
Beyoğlu ①

The only Roman Catholic Church to have been converted into a mosque, Arap Cami was once the 14th-century Church of San Domenico. Its peculiar name (which translates to 'Arab Mosque') comes from the deported Andalusian Arabs who were allowed to settle in the area after the Spanish Inquisition.

300 ZEYREK MOSQUE

Zeyrek Mh.
İbadethande Arkası Sk.
Fatih ②

Once a Byzantine monastery that was the largest church in Constantinople after Hagia Sophia, Zeyrek consists of three separate churches all built in the 12th century. With its many beautiful domes and a façade that exemplifies the Byzantine recessed-brick-technique, Zeyrek Cami is quite the find in the backstreets of a historic neighbourhood.

5 *gorgeous* HISTORIC APARTMENTS

301 **FREJ APARTMENT**
Şişhane Mh.
Corner of Okçu Musa Cd. (which later becomes Bankalar Cd.) & Büyük Hendek Cd.
Beyoğlu ①

This renovated beauty, which stands tall in the middle of Şişhane square (so-called by locals), always beckons a second glance because of its façade of sculptures and ornate decorative details. The apartment is believed to have been built in 1906 for Selim Hanna Frej by the architect Constantinos P. Kyriakides and abides to the German Jugendstil.

302 **GÜMÜŞSUYU APARTMENT**
Ömer Avni Mh.
İnönü Cd. 18
Beyoğlu ①

Believed to be a structure belonging to the early 19th century, the Gümüşsuyu Palas exudes a fabulous confluence of art nouveau and neo-baroque styles with an embellished façade of decorative mouldings nostalgic for Istanbul's rather elegant past.

303 **ARIF PAŞA APARTMENT**
İnönü Mh.
Elmadağ Cd. 12
Şişli ③

Built by the architect Constantin Pappa in 1902 for Arif Paşa (the Ottoman Empire's last court doctor), this historic apartment curves around a beautiful courtyard. Hidden away in the backstreets of Elmadağ, you can try to take a peek inside if the entrance door is open.

304 KAMONDO APARTMENT

Müeyyedzade Mh.
Serdar-ı Ekrem Cd. 22
Beyoğlu ①

The Sephardic Jewish Kamondo family of financiers and philanthropists are responsible for three notable structures: the Kamondo Stairs, Palace and this beautiful apartment near the Galata Tower. Built in the 19th century, the apartment allowed Avram Kamondo to easily stroll to his own bank on Bankalar Caddesi.

305 MISIR APARTMENT

Tomtom Mh.
İstiklal Cd. 163
Beyoğlu ①

Open to the public (due to the art galleries inside), Mısır Apartmanı was built between 1905–1910 by architect Hovsep Aznavuryan for Abbas Halim Paşa, the Egyptian Khedive's nephew. The art nouveau building was also once home to Turkish poet Mehmet Akif Ersoy, who famously wrote the Turkish national anthem.

302 GÜMÜŞSUYU APARTMENT

YENIKÖY

İSKELE
BALIK

70 PLACES TO DISCOVER ISTANBUL

5 *lesser-known*

GREEK ORTHODOX STRUCTURES

306 **CHURCH OF ST. GEORGE**

Yavuz Sultan Selim Mh.
Dr. Sadık Ahmet Cd. 44
Fatih ②
+90 212 531 96 70
patriarchate.org

Part of the Ecumenical Patriarchate of Constantinople compound (the symbolic base of the Greek Orthodox Church), the 19th-century Church of St. George is one of Istanbul's most important religious sites. Inside, the walnut candle stand with ivory petals and the beautifully restored iconostasis are just two details to be admired.

307 HALKI SEMINARY

307 HALKI SEMINARY

Heybeliada Mh.
Ümit Sk.
Adalar ⑧
+90 216 351 85 63
theologicalschool halki.com

At the very top of Heybeliada, Ruhban Okulu (Halki Seminary) was the Ecumenical Patriarchate of Constantinople's main school of theology opened in 1844. Forcibly closed in 1971 (due to a law that banned private higher education), the school, its chapel and the serene garden with a sea view have all remained impeccably intact.

308 CHURCH OF HAGIOS IOANNIS PRODROMOS

Yenice Sk. 3
Burgazada ⑧

The most prominent sight on Burgazada, the Church of Hagios Ioannis Prodromos (St. John the Baptist) was built in 1896 and towers above all else with its large dome. Built on the site of a 9th-century Byzantine monastery, the church is still an active part of the island's Greek community.

309 PHANAR GREEK ORTHODOX HIGH SCHOOL

Balat Mh.
Sancaktar Ykş. 36
Fatih ②
+90 212 521 22 52

Rising like a red castle above the mostly dilapidated landscape of the historic Balat neighbourhood, the Phanar Greek Orthodox High School has been educating its students since 1881. Built by the architect Konstantinos Dimadis, the school was made from a red brick specially imported from Marseille.

310 AYA YORGI CHURCH

Büyükada-Nizam Mh.
Cennet Yolu
Adalar ⑧

The steep climb to the top of Büyükada is very much worth it because of this historic Greek Orthodox monastery from the 6th century (as well as the amazing view). An important Christian pilgrimage site, the faithful climb their way to the church every year on April 23rd.

5 *beautiful*
OTTOMAN FOUNTAINS

311 **SULTAN II. ABDÜLHAMIT FOUNTAIN**
Harbiye Mh.
Maçka Cd.
Şişli ③

Located across the beautiful Istanbul Technical University building (built by Simon and Sarkis Balyan in 1861–1862), this Ottoman fountain was designed by Italian architect Raimondo D'Aronco in 1901 for Sultan II. Abdülhamit. A baroque beauty constructed entirely of marble, the fountain marks the Maçka Democracy Park entrance.

312 **TOPHANE MEYDAN FOUNTAIN**
Kılıçali Paşa Mh.
Meclis-i Mebusan Cd.
Beyoğlu ①

Istanbul's fountains hark back to a time when homes had no running water and residents relied on neighbourhood fountains for their daily tasks. The third largest of these fountains is the baroque Tophane Meydan Çeşmesi (Fountain), commissioned by Mahmud I and constructed by Mehmet Ağa in 1732 in ornately decorated marble.

312 **TOPHANE MEYDAN FOUNTAIN**

313 BEREKETZADE FOUNTAIN

**Bereketzade Mh.
Galata Kulesi 1
Beyoğlu ①**

Also a place for social interaction, one can imagine how people flocked to the Bereketzade Fountain to fill their containers and converse. Built in 1733, this wall fountain is one of the Tulip era's most beautiful and features similar flower and fruit motifs as seen in Ahmet III's Fruit Room in the Topkapı Palace.

314 AHMED III FOUNTAIN

**Sultan Ahmet Mh.
Soğuk Çeşme Sk.
Fatih ②**

Right by the Imperial Gate of Topkapı Palace, this grand structure was built in 1728-1729 in the place of an old Byzantine fountain. It's very much indicative of Ahmed III's reign, which spread its preference for magnificent decoration all over the city, including colourful arch stones, tiles, floral motifs and calligraphy.

315 İSHAK AĞA FOUNTAIN

**Merkez Mh.
Mehmet Yavuz Cd. 3
Beykoz ⑥**

Also known as the On Çeşmeler (Ten Fountains) this large roofed fountain in Beykoz Square with Ottoman-style arches and decorative details dates back to the 18th century and is believed to have healing powers. The plane tree next to it is also famous for being more than 280 years old.

The 5 places to
ESCAPE CROWDS

316 **BALAT KÜLTÜR EVI**
Balat Mh.
Vodina Cd. 39-41
Fatih ②
+90 212 531 00 57

A member of Soroptimist International (a global volunteer movement) Balat Kültür Evi aims to help women realise their career goals. Inside the beautifully renovated house, visitors can view exhibitions in the gallery and enjoy delicious homemade Turkish food in the cafe where women from the neighbourhood are employed and trained.

317 **ZANAAT ATELYE**
Tomtom Mh.
Boğazkesen Cd. 67
Beyoğlu ①

An arched doorway leads into the hidden courtyard of the neo-renaissance St. Eugène Palace, whose rooms are filled with the more than 300 moulds (representing every era of architectural history) belonging to Kemal Çimbiz, the city's last master plaster-caster.

318 **BAHÇEDE SINEK KAFE**
Büyükada-Maden Mh.
Yılmaztürk Cd. 110
Adalar ⑧
+90 216 382 35 78
bahcedesinek.com

A husband and wife duo who live in one of the island's most beautiful houses also decided to open a cafe right in their own garden. You'll want to spend hours here trying out their daily dishes, drinking coffee and taking a peak at their beautifully minimal-modern home.

319 YILDIZ PARK

Yıldız Mh.
Çırağan Cd.
Beşiktaş ③

Istanbul's largest park was once part of Yıldız Palace's imperial gardens. Even though the palace is no longer accessible, the park itself is open to all with its serene walking paths, a duck pond and the fantastic Malta Köşkü, an imperial neo-baroque kiosk built by Sarkis Balyan that is now a restaurant.

320 HEKIMOĞLU ALI PAŞA MOSQUE

Cerrahpaşa Mh.
Kızılelma Cd. 74
Fatih ②
+90 538 510 54 51

Past an arched gateway the garden of the Hekimoğlu Ali Paşa Mosque is a bit of true serenity in a city of millions. One of Istanbul's least known mosques (built between 1734 and 1735), Hekimoğlu Ali Paşa is considered one of the last works belonging to classical Turkish architecture.

319 YILDIZ PARK

5 *lovely historic* HANS

321 KURŞUNLU HAN

Arap Cami Mh.
Kardeşim Sk. 47
Beyoğlu ①

Istanbul's *hans* served as inns for travelling merchants who could rest and do business in these traditional caravanserais. The Kurşunlu Han, built in the 1540s for Süleyman the Magnificent's Grand Vizier, has some of the city's last remaining handicraftsmen workshops as well as the newer ateliers of young artists and designers.

322 ÖMER ABED HAN

Kemankeş Mh.
Kemankeş Cd.
Beyoğlu ①

Built in 1909 by Alexandre Vallaury, the Ömer Abed Han is like an updated caravanserai. Once a customs house with offices of upper middle class bureaucrats, today the run-down *han* is filled with electronic shops, hiding beautiful details such as ornate wrought iron railings and original tile flooring.

323 BÜYÜK VALIDE HAN

Mercan Mh.
Çakmakçılar Ykş. 31
Fatih ②

Built in the 17th century, the teeming days of commerce seem to echo faintly through the dark abandoned halls of the Büyük Valide Han. Visit the remaining artisan workshops and ask permission to visit the domed roof.

324 BÜYÜK YENI HAN

Taya Hatun Mh.
Çakmakçılar Ykş. 56
Fatih ②

Another dilapidated beauty that exudes a past vivacity, the Büyük Yeni Han was commissioned by Sultan Mustafa III and built by architect Mehmet Tahir Ağa in 1764. The upper floors with their stone masonry arches look down on the central courtyard where a few shops still go about their daily business.

325 ZINCIRLI HAN

Taya Hatun Mh.
Acı Çeşme Sk.
Mercan Gate
Fatih ②

One of the liveliest of the *hans*, the Zincirli Han's pink and white arched façade surrounds a cobble-stoned courtyard where a small teahouse serves up the daily orders. Artisan workshops and Şişko Osman's famous carpet shop are all reasons to visit this hidden secret from the late 18th century.

321 KURŞUNLU HAN

5
HIDDEN CHURCHES

326 BULGARIAN ST. STEPHEN CHURCH

Balat Mh.
Mürselpaşa Cd. 85
Fatih ②

One of the few surviving prefabricated cast iron churches in the world, the beautifully ornamented St. Stephen Church is a neo-Gothic and baroque stunner. Built in 1898, the church is composed of prefabricated parts that weigh around 500 tons, all produced in Vienna and transported to Istanbul.

326 BULGARIAN ST. STEPHEN CHURCH

327 CHRIST CHURCH

Hacımimi Mh.
Yazıcı Çk.
Beyoğlu ①
+90 212 455 59 00

Walk to the end of Serdar-ı Ekrem Street to discover this Anglican Church almost undetectable behind the trees. Built by the English architect George Edmund Street around 1858, the Gothic church was built as a memorial to the Crimean War. Spend some time admiring the altar and the serene garden.

328 ARMENIAN EVANGELICAL CHURCH

Kamer Hatun Mh.
Hamalbaşı Cd. 44
Beyoğlu ①

Hidden away in the low-income Tarlabaşı area, 'The First Armenian Evangelical Church of the World', was founded in 1846 by reformists who formed their own religious community after being excommunicated by the Armenian Patriarchate of Constantinople.

329 CHURCH OF PANAGIA EVANGELISTRIA

Yenişehir Mh.
Hacı İlbey Sk. 6
Beyoğlu ③

Two giant bell towers and a red dome rise above the dusty landscape of the chaotic Dolapdere area. The Greek Orthodox Church of Panagia Evangelistria dates back to 1894 and its phenomenal interior of frescoes, antique chandeliers and iconography can only be seen Sunday mornings during service.

330 HAGIA TRIADA GREEK ORTHODOX CHURCH

Katip Mustafa Çelebi Mh.
Meşelik Sk. 7
Beyoğlu ①

The imposing dome of Istanbul's largest Greek Orthodox Church hides behind the bustle of Taksim Square and only a few wander down the side streets to discover its beauty. Erected in 1880 and still used by the city's Greek community, Hagia Triada's interior is a breathtaking visual collection of marble designs and ornate paintings.

5 *innovative*

CITY TOUR GUIDES

331 **ISTANBUL TOUR STUDIO**
Levent Mh.
Mektep Sk. 10 1-1
Beşiktaş ④
+90 212 243 05 21
istanbultourstudio.com

Sinan Sökmen founded his boutique travel agency in 2013 so that travellers could see Istanbul through the eyes of connoisseurs and local experts. From helicopter tours to rowing on the Golden Horn, street photography walks to mushroom hunting, Sökmen and his guides cater to every travel need and interest.

332 **CULINARY WALKS WITH CULINARY BACKSTREETS**
culinary backstreets.com

Founded by Ansel Mullins and Yigal Schleifer in 2009, the website Culinary Backstreets focusses on Istanbul's lesser-known traditional culinary culture. Its Culinary Walks take on unique aspects of the city's vast food landscape such as the hidden eateries of Beyoğlu or three distinct Bosphorus neighbourhoods' food scenes.

333 LOCALLY ISTANBUL

AT: BOTANIK CARSI (OFFICE)

Atasehir Atatürk Mh.
Meric Cd. 15/38
Atasehir ⑨
+90 538 064 94 00
locallyistanbul.com

Ümit Aggül and Erk Erkaya, who founded Locally Istanbul in 2011, just want to show you the Istanbul where they were born and raised. Tailor-made tours delve into the vibrant worlds of design, fashion, art, culture, music and nightlife. Don't forget to ask about the special vintage motorcycle tour.

334 FEST TRAVEL

Barbaros Blv. 74,
Barbaros Apt. 20,
7th Fl.
Beşiktaş ③
+90 850 622 33 78
festtravel.com

Fest Travel caters to the more history-enthused travellers who want to delve deeper into Istanbul's fascinating story. Apart from tailor-made tours, the expert Fest Travel guides take on fascinating subjects such as art nouveau architecture, the city walls and gates, Byzantine history and Jewish Heritage (to name a few).

335 THE ARMADA BOAT

Cankurtaran Mh.
Ahırkapı Sk. 24
Fatih ②
+90 212 455 44 55
thearmadaboat.istanbul

Inspired by Istanbul's elegant early 20th-century excursion boats, Kasım Zoto (the owner of Armada Otel) and his team built the Armada Excursion Boat to bring back the days of touring the Bosphorus in style. The boat can be rented for refined Bosphorus, Golden Horn or Princes' Islands tours with food and cocktails.

5 of the best
TURKISH BATHS

336 **KILIÇ ALI PAŞA HAMAM**
Kemankeş Mh.
Hamam Sk. 1
Beyoğlu ①
+90 212 393 80 10
kilicalipasa hamami.com

Part of the Kılıç Ali Paşa Mosque complex, it took seven years to renovate this hamam built by Mimar Sinan between 1578–1583. Spend a few moments admiring the majestic main dome before wrapping yourself in a soft *peştamal* towel and heading to your cleansing hamam treatment at one of Istanbul's cleanest and most professional hamams.

337 **ÇUKURCUMA HAMAM**
Firuzağa Mh.
Çukurcuma Cd. 43
Beyoğlu ①
+90 212 243 64 80
cukurcuma hamami.com

After a long and meticulous period of renovation the beautiful Çukurcuma Hamamı, which dates back to 1830, opened in September 2018 as a boutique Turkish bath. Apart from the traditional body scrubbing and bubble wash, visitors can also opt for a massage with organic oils and a hand and foot peeling treatment.

339 ÇAĞALOĞLU HAMAM

338 AYASOFYA HÜRREM SULTAN HAMAM

Cankurtaran Mh.
Ayasofya Meydanı 2
Fatih ②
+90 212 517 35 35
ayasofyahamami.com

This hamam was built between 1556–1557 by Mimar Sinan under the order of Hürrem Sultan, the wife of Sultan Süleyman the Magnificent. After being used as a jail, a storage space and later as a carpet bazaar, the hamam was finally brought back to its former glory and use in 2008.

339 ÇAĞALOĞLU HAMAM

Alemdar Mh.
Prof. Kazım İsmail Gürkan Cd. 34
Fatih ②
+90 212 522 24 24
cagaloglu hamami.com.tr

One of Istanbul's most beautiful hamams, Çağaloğlu was commissioned by Sultan Mahmut I and constructed in 1741 by architects Süleyman Ağa and Abdullah Ağa. The last hamam to be built during the Ottoman era, Çağaloğlu features grand marble columns, decorative fountains and domed ceilings that let the natural light trickle through.

340 ÇEMBERLITAŞ HAMAM

Mollafenari Mh.
Vezirhan Cd. 8
Fatih ②
+90 212 522 79 74
cemberlitas hamami.com

Another beautiful hamam by Mimar Sinan, Çemberlitaş was built in 1584 on the order of Nurbanu Sultan, the wife of Selim II, to raise funds for the Valide-i Atik Mosque in Üsküdar. The hamam gets its name from Çemberlitaş, the Roman monumental Column of Constantine.

The 5 most notable
SHOPPING ARCADES

341 **HAK PASAJI**
Teşvikiye Mh.
Teşvikiye Cd. 22
Şişli ③

The Hak Pasajı is home to tailors, watchmakers, stamp collectors and, most notably, the Orlando Carlo Calumeno shop downstairs. Travel back to Turkey in the 19th and early 20th centuries with beautiful antique objects of daily life as well as an astounding collection of Ottoman postcards.

342 **HAZZOPULO PASAJI**
Asmalı Mescit Mh.
İstiklal Cd. 116
Beyoğlu ①

Underneath a delicate roof of vines and tree branches, the courtyard of the Hazzopulo Pasajı is always alive with people drinking tea, playing backgammon or just curiously wandering about. Built in 1871 by the Greek Hacopulo family of bankers, this particular *pasaj* was famously frequented by the Ottoman author Ahmet Mithat Efendi and the Young Turks.

343 **SURIYE PASAJI**
Asmalı Mescit Mh.
İstiklal Cd. 166
Beyoğlu ①

With beautiful neoclassical details that unfurl in the lamplight, this arcade gets its name from the Syrian Hasan Halbuni Paşa who commissioned it to the architect Demetre Th. Bassiladis in 1908.

344 ÇIÇEK PASAJI

Hüseyinağa Mh.
İstiklal Cd. 80
Beyoğlu ①

When the Naum Theatre (which hosted Verdi's *Il Trovatore* before the Paris opera houses) burned down in 1876, Greek banker Hristaki Zoğrafos Efendi commissioned architect Kleanthis Zannos to build the Cité de Péra. The arcade got its present name ('Flower Arcade') from the impoverished noble Russian women who sold flowers there after the Russian Revolution.

345 AVRUPA PASAJI

Hüseyinağa Mh.
Meşrutiyet Cd. 8
Beyoğlu ①

Past the decorative marble and wrought-iron entrance of this neo-renaissance arcade, 22 stores (mostly selling lovely antiques) stretch down one passageway underneath a glass roof. Built in 1874 by the architect Domenico Pulgher, the arcade's upper levels are decorated with sculptures and Corinthian columns.

341 HAK PASAJI

5 spots to

TAKE IN THE VIEW

346 **CHRIST HILL – BURGAZADA**

Burgazada Mh.
Follow dirt path past Büyük Çamlık Sk.
Adalar ⑧

A sense of penetrating serenity is inevitable when you reach the top of Burgazada overlooking the expanse of the sea and horizon. The Hristos Tepesi (Christ Hill) was once home to a Byzantine monastery, but nowadays only ruins and a small 19th-century church remain, as well as the fascinating Greek cemetery amid the pines.

346 CHRIST HILL – BURGAZADA

347 **YAVUZ SULTAN SELIM MOSQUE**
Balat Mh.
Sultan Selim Cd. 18
Fatih ②
+90 212 599 34 77

Built between 1522 and 1529, this mosque is dedicated to the infamous Selim I who killed more than a few of his family members in order to guarantee his and his son Süleyman the Magnificent's ascension to the throne. Located on Istanbul's fifth hill, the mosque's terrace looks out over a gorgeous Golden Horn view.

348 **5. KAT**
Cihangir Mh.
Soğancı Sk. 3, 5th Fl.
Beyoğlu ①
+90 212 293 37 74
5kat.com

Owned by the Turkish actress Yasemin Alkaya, 5. Kat (5th Floor) has been a favourite among the Cihangir neighbourhood's intellectual crowd since 1993. Of course, the fantastic Bosphorus view from the terrace, as well as live musical performances, are some additional reasons why locals keep coming back.

349 **KALPAZANKAYA**
Burgazada Mh.
Kalpazankaya Yolu Sk. 42
Adalar ⑧
+90 216 381 11 11
kalpazankaya.com.tr

Another hidden beauty on the lovely island of Burgaz, Kalpazankaya's simple wooden tables and chairs look out over a beautiful view of the sea underneath the shade of pine trees. A great place to grab a simple lunch while exploring the island or for watching the sunset.

350 **RUMELI FENERI CASTLE**
Rumelifeneri Mh.
Sarıyer ⑥

Located on Istanbul's northernmost point, the quiet fishing village of Rumeli Feneri, with its casual seafood eateries, is a wonder completely removed from city life. The nearby 17th-century Rumeli Feneri Castle, built by Sultan Murad IV for surveillance purposes, looks out over the wild open sea.

5 places to go with the KIDS

351 ATATÜRK ARBORETUM
AT: ISTANBUL UNIVERSITY – FACULTY OF FORESTRY
Kemer Mh.
Sarıyer ⑥
+90 212 226 19 29

When Istanbul's hectic energy becomes a bit overwhelming, wind down in the 296-hectare Atatürk Arboretum filled with more than 1500 plant species from all over the world. Established in 1949 and named after Atatürk in 1982 (on his 100th birthday), the long walking paths wind through the flora and lakes.

352 ISTANBUL TOY MUSEUM
Göztepe Mh.
Dr. Zeki Zeren Sk. 15
Kadıköy ⑨
+90 216 359 45 50
istanbuloyuncak muzesi.com

Founded by the Turkish poet Sunay Akın in 2005, Turkey's only private toy museum is housed in a lovely Ottoman mansion with more than 4000 toys from the 1700s to the present. Antique toys from all over the world are displayed in specially designed themed rooms.

353 **ISTANBUL NAVAL MUSEUM**

Sinanpaşa Mh.
Beşiktaş Cd. 6-1
Beşiktaş ③
+90 212 327 43 45
denizmuzesi.dzkk.tsk.tr

Befittingly situated next to the public square that commemorates the famous Ottoman admiral Barbaros Hayrettin Paşa, the Istanbul Naval Museum was established in 1961 but underwent a five-year renovation reopening in 2013. The modern three-storey museum has a mesmerising collection of imperial wooden rowboats and caïques and other maritime beauties of yore.

354 **EMIRGAN PARK**

Reşitpaşa Mh.
Emirgan Sk.
Sarıyer ⑥

One of Istanbul's largest parks, the Emirgan Korusu (Park) changed hands many times during the centuries and was last owned by Khedive Ismail Paşa who built three historic wooden mansions that survive to this day. With its decorative ponds and blooming flora, the park is especially popular during the Tulip Festival (first week of April).

355 **ISTANBUL AVIATION MUSEUM**

Yeşilköy Mh.
Eski Havaalanı Cd.
Bakırköy ⑨
+90 212 663 24 90
istanbulmuze.hvkk.tsk.tr

Established in the 1960s and located near the Atatürk Airport, the Istanbul Aviation Museum explores the Turkish Air Force's history. Most notable is the fascinating outdoor exhibition area where German-made planes used during WWI as well as captured foreign aircrafts seem to be ready for take-off.

The 5 loveliest

OTTOMAN PAVILIONS

356 **TOPHANE PAVILION**
Kılıçali Paşa Mh.
Meclis-i Mebusan Cd. 2
Beyoğlu ①

Sultan Abdülmecit commissioned the English architect William James Smith (who also designed the Dolmabahçe Palace's beautiful Glass Pavilion) to construct this exquisite baroque house in a shade of seafoam-green and white. Constructed between 1851–1852, the pavilion was used for the visits of foreign statesmen and is nowadays part of the Mimar Sinan Fine Arts University.

357 **IHLAMUR PAVILION**
Teşvikiye Mh.
Muradiye Bostanı Cd.
Beşiktaş ③

Constructed during the reign of Sultan Abdülmecid I, the two beautifully ornate baroque mansions of the Ihlamur Kasrı complex were designed by the architect Nikogos Balyan between 1849 and 1855. Once a place of sojourn in the countryside, the mansions and their garden are now sheltered by a wall from the busy traffic outside.

358 KÜÇÜKSU PAVILION

Göksu Mh.
Küçüksu Cd.
Beykoz ⑥

Built in 1857 and overlooking the Bosphorus, the Küçüksu Kasrı (Pavilion) was built by Sultan Abdülmecid as a place to rest during hunting excursions. Inside the opulent mansion, which is now a museum, lavish furniture, carpets and art from Europe decorate every inch, including grand chandeliers that hang from the ceilings.

359 HIDIV PAVILION

Çubuklu Mh.
Piri Reis Cd. 32
Beykoz ⑥
+90 216 331 23 42
hidivkasri.com

Commissioned by Abbas Hilmi Paşa, the last Khedive (Viceroy) of Egypt, to the Italian architect Delfo Seminati, the Hıdiv (Khedive / Viceroy) Palace was completed in 1907. An art nouveau beauty with a prominent tower, the palace is now run as a restaurant and cafe.

360 ABDÜLMECID EFENDI MANSION

Kuzguncuk Mh.
Kuşbakışı Cd. 16
Üsküdar ⑤
+90 216 343 36 76
ktsk.com.tr

A breathtaking example of late 19th-century Ottoman architecture, this mansion was Egyptian Khedive İsmail Paşa's hunting lodge before becoming Abdülmecid Efendi's summerhouse. Once a meeting place for artists and writers, the mansion now stands idly in its magnificence inside the Koç Sports Club.

5 essential activities on the
ASIAN SIDE

361 **ADMIRE THE BULL STATUE**
Osmanağa Mh.
Söğütlü Çeşme Cd. 61
Kadıköy ⑦

Made by sculptor Isidore Bonheur in 1864, the Bull Statue (Boğa Heykeli) travelled from Alsace-Lorraine to the German Empire during the Franco-Prussian War and was later given to Ottoman General Enver Paşa as a gift from German Kaiser Wilhelm II. After decorating the Yıldız Palace and later the Hilton Hotel, the statue finally arrived in Kadıköy in 1970.

362 **RIDE THE NOSTALGIC T3 TRAM**
Caferağa Mah.
Kadıköy IDO Station
Kadıköy ⑦
metro.istanbul

Travel back in time to a pre-1956 Istanbul where a large tramway network transported people to and fro. Nowadays, only two of these tramlines exist, one on Istiklal, and the other on the Kadıköy to Moda nostalgic route completed regularly by a lovely secondhand Tatra GT6 from Germany.

363 **GAZE AT THE SARICA ARIF PAŞA MANSION**
Caferağa Mh.
Moda Cd. 233
Kadıköy ⑦

Hiding its neoclassical beauty behind its gates and away from Moda Caddesi's bustle of modern venues, this mansion was once surrounded by a sprawling garden. Completed by architect Constantine P. Pappa in 1903, the mansion remains as a beautiful reminder of the past.

364 **EAT AT KOÇO**
Caferağa Mh.
Moda Cd. 171
Kadıköy ⑦
+90 216 336 07 95
kocorestaurant.net

Open since 1928, Koço is one of Kadıköy's oldest restaurants and almost every resident has a few memories associated with this *rakı*, meze and fish institution. Reserve a terrace table overlooking the water and definitely visit the Orthodox shrine and sacred spring in the basement.

365 **DISCOVER THE AYA TRIADA CHURCH**
Caferağa Mh.
Hacı Şükrü Sk. 17
Kadıköy ⑦

Established in 1902, the large and beautiful Greek Orthodox Church of the Holy Trinity is pretty much hidden away in the residential backstreets. Stroll around its lovely garden and venture inside to admire the finely painted iconostasis of this neo-Byzantine and neo-renaissance church built by the architects G. Zahariadis and Belissarios Makropoulos.

361 ADMIRE THE BULL STATUE

5 neighbourhoods perfect for WANDERING

366 KUZGUNCUK

Kuzguncuk Mh.
Üsküdar ⑤

Kuzguncuk is as nostalgic as it is multicultural with its historic synagogues, churches and mosques and rows of colourful 19th-century Ottoman houses. Charming bookstores, cafes and restaurants line İcadiye Street, and Kuzguncuk even has a garden where residents grow their own organic produce.

367 BALAT AND FENER

Balat and Fener Mh.
Fatih ②

Dilapidated yet beautiful row houses and countless historic churches and synagogues belong to the former neighbourhood of upper-class Greeks (Fener) and the Jewish quarter (Balat). Nowadays the neighbourhoods are full of trendy cafes and restaurants established by Istanbul's young and talented entrepreneurs.

368 YENIKÖY

Yeniköy Mh.
Sarıyer ⑨

A neighbourhood famous for its beautiful *yalı* (waterfront mansions), fish restaurants and hidden historic churches and synagogues, Yeniköy has a lot to explore on foot. Once a mostly Greek neighbourhood, notable remnants include the Yeniköy Panagia Greek Orthodox Church and the Greek Orthodox Elementary School.

369 **MODA**
Moda Mh.
Kadıköy ⑦

Moda is young and bohemian and if it had an anthem it would be a song by the late Barış Manço, a Kadıköy native and one of the pioneers of the 1970s era psychedelic Anatolian rock movement. Explore the many shops, bars, and cafes in and around Moda Caddesi (Street), and take a stroll on the waterside boardwalk.

370 **TEŞVIKIYE**
Teşvikiye Mh.
Şişli ③

There's constantly something new opening up in Teşvikiye, a neighbourhood of cool shops, cafes, restaurants and bars scattered among charming historic apartments. The best place to explore is the area behind the Teşvikiye mosques and some favourites include the Vesaire florist and the Ela Cindoruk jewellery shop.

366 **KUZGUNCUK**

5

HISTORIC GEMS

hiding in plain sight

371 BRITISH SEAMEN'S HOSPITAL

Bereketzade Mh.
Bereketzade Cami Sk. 2
Beyoğlu ①
+90 212 251 59 00

Built in 1903 by the English architect Charles Holden, this hospital's massive scale conveys how important Istanbul was for British naval passage. Currently used as an eye hospital, the iron gates still bear the initials 'BSH', and from afar, the large tower is as visually prominent as the Galata Tower.

372 CHURCH OF SAINTS PETER AND PAUL

Bereketzade Mh.
Galata Kulesi Sk. 44
Beyoğlu ①

Dating back to the 15th century, this church was reconstructed in 1843 by the Swiss-Italian architect brothers Gaspare and Giuseppe Fossati who are most famous for having restored the Hagia Sophia for Sultan Abdülmecid I. Inside the beautiful altar the cupola in blue shines with golden stars.

373 FERIKÖY PROTESTANT CEMETERY

Cumhuriyet Mh.
Abide-i Hürriyet Cd. 5
Şişli ③

Renowned names such as Swiss scholar Ernest Mamboury, German musician Paul Lange and American photographer Josephine Powell rest in this beautifully overgrown historic cemetery. The Catholic Cemetery across the street is sadly not open to the public.

374 MAHMUT MUHTAR PAŞA MANSION

Caferağa Mh.
Hacı İzzet Sk. 7
Kadıköy ⑦
+90 216 345 09 71

Only viewable from the outside, the beautiful neoclassic 'Mermer Köşk' (Marble Mansion) was built in the 1870s for Mahmut Muhtar Paşa and his family. After being donated to the Ministry of Education, it served as a girls' school until being damaged in the 1999 earthquake and still awaits renovation.

375 CHURCH OF ST. MARY DRAPERIS

Tomtom Mh.
İstiklal Cd. 215
Beyoğlu ①
+90 212 244 02 43

Down the steps and past a beautiful neoclassical façade, the Church of St. Mary Draperis has an astonishing interior with barrel-vaulted ceilings that are entirely covered in paintings. Dating back to 1584, St. Mary Draperis enjoyed the status of being one of Istanbul's most prestigious Catholic churches during the 19th century.

371 BRITISH SEAMEN'S HOSPITAL

SÜREYYA OPERA HOUSE

45 PLACES TO ENJOY CULTURE

The 5 most unique

CULTURAL CENTRES

376 **SANTRALISTANBUL**
Emniyettepe Mh.
Kazım Karabekir
Cd. 2
Eyüp ⑨
+90 212 311 78 09
santralistanbul.org

After meticulous renovation and conversion, the Ottoman Empire's first power plant became one of Istanbul's most fascinating art and culture hubs. santralistanbul won the International Architecture Award in 2010 with its Main Gallery (featuring exhibition spaces as well as dining and entertainment venues) and the Energy Museum inside the plant's original turbine rooms.

377 **BEYKOZ KUNDURA**
Yalıköy Mh.
Süreyya İlmen Cd. 1
Beykoz ⑥
+90 216 323 31 30
beykozkundura.com

A huge leather shoe factory from the 1930s that has been in use as a film set since 2005, Beykoz Kundura opened to the public as Kundura Sinema when the former boiler room was converted into a cinema and events space that hosts regular film screenings and events.

376 SANTRALISTANBUL

378 YELDEĞIRMENI ARTS CENTRE

Rasimpaşa Mh.
İskele Sk. 43
Kadıköy ⑦
+90 216 337 00 58
yelsanat.kadikoy.bel.tr

Restored in 2013, the Yeldeğirmeni Sanat (Arts Centre) was once the Notre Dame du Rosaire Church, which belonged to the Sainte-Euphemie middle school. Music, theatre and other artistic events are held regularly in the French church's beautiful main sanctuary with stained-glass windows and hand-painted wall decorations.

379 TOPHANE-I AMIRE CULTURE AND ART CENTER

Kılıçali Paşa Mh.
Defterdar Ykş. 2
Beyoğlu ①
+90 212 293 46 48

The centre of the Ottoman weaponry industry, the Tophane (Armoury) quarter is home to Tophane-i Amire, a cannon ball casting factory built under the reign of Sultan Mehmet II. In 1992, the beautifully domed structure was transferred to the Mimar Sinan University and is used as an arts and culture centre with three exhibition halls.

380 SALT GALATA

Arap Cami Mh.
Bankalar Cd. 11
Beyoğlu ①
+90 212 334 22 00
saltonline.org

Inside the magnificent 19th-century Imperial Ottoman Bank building, SALT Galata is the ultimate cultural centre with a modern research library, bookstore, cafe, exhibition space, auditorium, the Ottoman Bank museum and the restaurant Neolokal. SALT Beyoğlu on İstiklal 136 is a fantastic three-floor exhibition space with a bookshop, cinema and winter garden.

5 excellent

CONTEMPORARY ART GALLERIES

381 **GALERIST**
Asmalı Mescit Mh.
Meşrutiyet Cd. 67,
1st Fl.
Beyoğlu ①
+90 212 252 18 96
galerist.com.tr

One of Istanbul's leading contemporary art galleries, Galerist has nurtured the careers of Turkey's most talented contemporary artists and introduced them to the world at leading art fairs. Located in a beautiful 18th-century building, Galerist also has another gallery in Hasköy in a former yarn factory from the 1950s.

382 **PILEVNELI GALLERY**
Yenişehir Mh.
Irmak Cd. 25
Beyoğlu ③
+90 212 259 03 94
pilevneli.com

Pilevneli's modern dark-grey-concrete façade serves as discernible evidence that the Dolapdere neighbourhood is slowly turning into Istanbul's new centre of arts. Designed by Emre Arolat Architects in 2017, the five-storey gallery is the latest project by Murat Pilevneli who established Galerist in 2001 and founded *IstanbulArtNews*, a leading local arts and culture publication.

383 **DIRIMART DOLAPDERE**

Hacıahmet Mh.
Irmak Cd. 1-9
Beyoğlu ③
+90 212 232 66 66
dirimart.com

Another very modern addition to Dolapdere, Dirimart's second gallery was designed by the German-Iranian architect and founder of New York based Studio MDA, Markus Dochantschi. Established by Hazer Özil in 2002, Dirimart quickly became one of Istanbul's leading contemporary art galleries mostly working with established Turkish artists.

384 **ARTER**

Dolapdere Mh.
Irmak Caddesi 13
Beyoğlu ①
+90 212 708 58 00
arter.org.tr

Designed by the London-based firm Grimshaw Architects, Arter's new location has Istanbul's first permanent collection of contemporary art. On six floors, with a total space of more than 18.000 square metres, 1300 works from more than 300 Turkish and international artists are on display and can be admired without paying an entrance fee.

385 **BORUSAN CONTEMPORARY ART GALLERY**

Rumeli Hisarı Mh.
Balta Limanı Hisar Cd. 5
Sarıyer ⑥
+90 212 393 52 00
borusan contemporary.com

Like a fairy-tale castle in red overlooking the Bosphorus, the former Yusuf Ziya Pasha Mansion built in 1911 now houses the offices of Borusan Holding. On weekends, however, the building is open to visitors as the Borusan Contemporary art gallery with a shop, cafe and terrace with amazing views.

5
LESSER-KNOWN MUSEUMS

386 **ARA GÜLER MUSEUM**
AT: BOMONTIADA
Merkez Mh.
Birahane Sk. 1
Şişli ③
+90 212 335 95 95
aragulermuzesi.com

Known as 'The Eye of Istanbul', the illustrious photojournalist Ara Güler is most famous for his iconic black and white images of a bygone Istanbul. The late photographer's museum takes an in-depth look at his pioneering 70-year career through photographs, notes, sketches and personal objects.

387 **THE QUINCENTENNIAL FOUNDATION MUSEUM OF TURKISH JEWS**
Bereketzade Mh.
Büyük Hendek Cd. 39
Beyoğlu ①
+90 212 292 63 33
muze500.com

Inside the beautiful Neve Şalom synagogue compound, this museum celebrates the culture and history of Istanbul's Jewish and Sephardic Jewish communities through objects, photographs and film. If you're lucky and a religious service is taking place during your visit, you can watch from the glass partition that separates the historic synagogue from the modern museum.

389 NATIONAL PALACES PAINTING MUSEUM

388 DOĞANÇAY MUSEUM

Hüseyinağa Mh.
Balo Sk. 42
Beyoğlu ①
+90 212 244 77 70
dogancaymuseum.org

Burhan Doğançay gave up his diplomatic career in 1964 to focus entirely on his fascination with urban walls, which inspired his greatest artworks and made him one of Turkey's most important contemporary artists. Inside a beautiful historic apartment, the Doğançay Museum exhibits the artist's work as well as that of his father, the famous painter Adil Doğançay.

389 NATIONAL PALACES PAINTING MUSEUM

Vişnezade Mh.
Dolmabahçe Cd.
Beşiktaş ③
+90 212 236 90 00
millisaraylar.gov.tr

Inside the opulent rooms of the Dolmabahçe Palace's former Crown Prince Residences, more than 200 paintings from the collections of various Ottoman palaces radiate their beauty under the light of antique chandeliers. On display are the works of Ottoman and Turkish artists, court painters, European artists and orientalist painters.

390 SADBERK HANIM MUSEUM

Büyükdere Mh.
Piyasa Cd. 27
Sarıyer ⑥
+90 212 242 38 13
sadberkhanimmuzesi.org.tr

Two beautiful 19th-century wooden villas exhibit the vast private collection of Sadberk Hanım (wife of Turkish entrepreneur Vehbi Koç) as well as the famous collector Hüseyin Kocabaş. More than 20.000 pieces on display range from Anatolian archaeological relics to Ottoman woven textiles, embroideries, garments and much more.

5 places to learn about
TURKISH HISTORY & CULTURE

391 **ANAMED**
AT: KOÇ UNIVERSITY-RESEARCH CENTER FOR ANATOLIAN CIVILIZATIONS
Tomtom Mh.
İstiklal Cd. 181
Beyoğlu ①
+90 212 393 60 00
rcac.ku.edu.tr

A wealth of information for serious Turkish history scholars, Koç University's research centre spans from prehistory to the end of the Ottoman era within various disciplines from archaeology to art history and more. Its exhibitions are therefore always fascinating, often displaying never-before-seen archival photography or documents that illuminate Turkey's multifaceted past.

392 **PERA MUSEUM**
Asmalı Mescit Mh.
Meşrutiyet Cd. 65
Beyoğlu ①
+90 212 334 99 00
peramuzesi.org.tr

Explore the worlds of orientalist paintings, Anatolian weights and measures and Kütahya tiles and ceramics as permanent exhibitions at the Pera Museum. Once the Bristol Hotel (built by architect Achille Manoussos in 1893) the modern museum has also hosted the work of illustrious international artists such as Picasso, Rembrandt and Goya.

393 ISTANBUL RESEARCH INSTITUTE

Asmalı Mescit Mh.
Meşrutiyet Cd. 47
Beyoğlu ①
+90 212 334 09 00
iae.org.tr

Part of the Pera Museum (but housed in another renovated 19th-century building), the Istanbul Research Institute delves deeper into Istanbul's Byzantine, Ottoman and Republican periods. Apart from its library (open to the public), the institute hosts local and international conferences as well as exhibitions.

394 SAKIP SABANCI MUSEUM

Emirgan Mh.
Sakıp Sabancı Cd. 42
Sarıyer ⑥
+90 212 277 22 00
sakipsabanci muzesi.org

In 1998, the Sabancı family turned their stunning estate and its lush garden (originally built by Italian architect Edoardo De Nari in 1925) into a museum. Today, the SSM's permanent collection includes Sakıp Sabancı's beautiful amassment of Islamic calligraphy and early Turkish paintings. Temporary exhibitions have also famously hosted the works of Picasso, Rodin and Ai Weiwei.

395 TURKISH AND ISLAMIC ARTS MUSEUM

Sultan Ahmet Mh.
Meydanı Sk. 46
Fatih ②
+90 212 518 18 05

A former Ottoman palace (built for Süleyman the Magnificent's Grand Vizier İbrahim Paşa in 1524) now houses one of the world's finest collections of carpets. The museum also has an outstanding collection of Islamic calligraphy as well as Islamic art painting, abstract and contemporary works.

The 5 essential

CITY FESTIVALS

396 **ISTANBUL INTERNATIONAL LITERATURE FESTIVAL**
Various locations
itef.com.tr

The first and only international literature festival in Turkey, ITEF has hosted more than 400 writers from 48 countries since its inception in 2009. A bookworm paradise, the festival hosts a spectrum of events from panels to spoken word performances to poetry readings and much more at select venues all over the city.

397 **FOTOISTANBUL**
Various locations
+90 212 444 44 55
fotoistanbul.org

Turkey's largest international photography festival, Fotoistanbul is known for its creative exhibition tactics that prefer to present photography out on the streets rather than in galleries. The festival exhibits works from local and international names, from the young to the established, as part of every day life, and open to all viewers.

398 FILMEKIMI
Various locations
filmekimi.iksv.org

One of the only opportunities to see independent and art house-style films at select Istanbul cinemas, Filmekimi has consistently brought film festival winners and new productions to the city's ardent cinephiles. From Godard to Lanthimos, Akın to Wenders, October is all about films.

399 IKSV MUSIC FESTIVAL
Various locations
iksv.org

The Istanbul Foundation for Culture and Arts (which also hosts the renowned Film, Jazz and Theatre Festivals) has brought the world's most prestigious orchestras, conductors, soloists and dance companies to Istanbul every year since 1973. The New York Philharmonic, Anne-Sophie Mutter and the Bolshoi Ballet are just some of the names.

400 IKSV ISTANBUL BIENNIAL
Various locations
+90 212 334 07 00
iksv.org

Held every two years since 1987 with a curator selected by an international advisory board, the Biennial turns Istanbul into a meeting point between audience and visual art from diverse cultural backgrounds. In the past, art installations have appeared on the streets, and historic private venues were opened to the public as exhibition spaces.

5 *very unique* CULTURAL EXPERIENCES

401 **GALATA MEVLEVI MUSEUM**
Şahkulu Mh.
Galip Dede Cd. 15
Beyoğlu ①
+90 212 245 41 41
galatamevlevihanesi muzesi.gov.tr

Become entranced by the whirling dervishes' fluttering white garbs as they glide perfectly along the oval stage. Built in 1491, the Mevlevihane (Mevlevi Lodge) has been a Sufism (Islamic mysticism) museum since 1975 and hosts daily whirling dervish ceremonies. Get there early to grab a seat right by the stage.

402 **HISTORIC TIMBER HOUSES**
Zeyrek Mh.
Fatih ②

Explore the area around Süleymaniye Mosque and the Zeyrek neighbourhood to discover Istanbul's wooden vernacular homes from the late 19th century. Still beautiful in their modesty, the UNESCO World Heritage listed timber abodes are the last physical reminders of the simple life outside the Ottoman palaces.

403 SÜREYYA OPERA HOUSE

Caferağa Mh.
Bahariye Cd. 29
Kadıköy ⑦
+90 216 346 15 31
sureyyaoperasi.kadikoy.bel.tr

Istanbul's only historic opera house, the Süreyya Operası was established by Süreyya İlmen Pasha in 1927 and continues to present a full program of performances on its main stage underneath an antique chandelier surrounded by delicate frescoes. With the unsettling demolition of the Atatürk Cultural Centre, the Süreyya Operası has become even more cherished.

404 DEPO

Tophane Mh.
Lüleci Hendek Cd. 12
Beyoğlu ①
+90 212 292 39 56
depoistanbul.net

Housed in a former tobacco warehouse, DEPO is much more than an art gallery, hosting screenings, panel discussions, workshops and presentations that allow politically and socially engaged projects to come to fruition. A platform for the exchange of ideas, DEPO also publishes the online journal *Red Thread*.

405 SCHNEIDERTEMPEL ART CENTER

Bereketzade Mh.
Felek Sk. 1
Beyoğlu ①
+90 212 249 01 50
schneidertempel.org

One of the three synagogues established by the area's Ashkenazi Jews during the 19th century, Schneidertempel was converted into an art centre in 1998 with a focus on contemporary caricature artists. The main sanctuary, with its Star of David stained-glass windows and antique chandeliers, is now the main exhibition hall.

5 places to discover

STREET ART & MUSIC

406 **YELDEĞIRMENI**
Karakolhane Cd.
Kadıköy ⑦

In 2012, the founders of the Mural Istanbul Festival decided to turn the agonisingly plain apartment building façades in their neighbourhood into giant canvases for street art. Explore the İskele, Uzun Hafız and Misaki Milli Streets to gaze up admiringly at large-scale murals that were created by local and international street artists during the annual festival.

407 **SARIYER**

407 **SARIYER**
Büyükdere Mh.
Çayıbaşı Cd.
Sarıyer ⑥

In 2018, the Mural Istanbul Festival travelled from Kadıköy to Sarıyer to turn another neighbourhood into an open-air exhibition of excellent street art. Explore Çayıbaşı Street to discover the large-scale murals of the local street artists Max on Duty, Leo Lunatic and Esk Reyn.

408 **OSMANBEY METRO STOP**
Corner of Halaskargazi Cd. and Rumeli Cd.
Şişli ③

Find the official Istanbul metro music spot (designated with a music-themed wall decal) by following the 'Rumeli', exit at the Osmanbey stop. Expect to come across a violin and cello duo, a remarkable solo guitarist with a voice like Elvis or a master of the traditional Turkish *kanun* instrument.

409 **ŞIŞHANE METRO**
Şişhane
Beyoğlu ①

A much less crowded (and appreciated) music spot is definitely hidden upstairs at the Şişhane metro stop. Take the 'İstiklal Caddesi' exit, and make a small contribution to a very talented jazz saxophonist or a man playing old Anatolian folk songs on his *saz* instrument.

410 **İSTIKLAL CADDESI**
İstiklal Cd.
Beyoğlu ①

Head to the famously overcrowded İstiklal Caddesi (Avenue) early in the morning (when it's not overcrowded) to really appreciate the beauty of its historic buildings, shopping arcades and the multitude of street art all around from local and international artists. To enjoy the street music, however, you'll have to come by later and brace the crowds.

5
UNUSUAL MUSEUMS

411 **AŞIYAN MUSEUM**
Bebek Mh.
Aşiyan Yokuşu
Beşiktaş ④
+90 212 263 69 86
istanbulkulturturizm.gov.tr

This beautiful villa built in 1906 was the former home of the famous Turkish poet Tevfik Fikret, considered to be the founder of modern Turkish poetry. Overlooking an inspiring view of the Bosphorus, the museum displays the personal belongings of Fikret and other writers of the 'Edebiyat-ı Cedide' (New Literature) movement.

412 **BARIŞ MANÇO MUSEUM**
Caferağa Mh.
Yusuf Kamil Paşa Sk. 5
Kadıköy ⑦
+90 216 337 94 13
barismanco.kadikoy.bel.tr

In the 1970s Barış Manço emerged as one of the pioneers of Anatolian Rock, a confluence of traditional Turkish folk and arabesque with the era's western rock influence. One of Turkey's most beloved musicians, Manço's former home is now a museum where everything from his Steinway piano to his iconic stage costumes are on display.

413 TÜRVAK MUSEUM

Tomtom Mh.
Yeni Çarşı Cd. 24
Beyoğlu ①
+90 212 245 80 91
turvak.com

Established in 2001 by TÜRVAK (a charitable foundation created by the Turkish director and producer Türker İnanoğlu in 1966) this museum is all about the 100-year history of Turkish cinema. Films, filming equipment, costumes, decoration, posters and photographs offer a comprehensive glimpse into the world of Turkish cinema as well as theatre.

414 ISTANBUL RAILWAY MUSEUM

Hoca Paşa Mh.
Sirkeci İstasyon Cd.
Fatih ②
+90 212 520 65 75

Built by the German architect August Jasmund in 1890, the Sirkeci Station is a beauty to behold and inside you'll find a small one-room museum that pays homage to the Orient Express. The Istanbul Railway Museum displays documents, objects and train artefacts belonging to the famously luxurious railway service that travelled from Paris to Istanbul.

415 URAL ATAMAN CLASSIC CAR MUSEUM

Ferahevler Mh.
Nuri Paşa Cd. 107
Sarıyer ⑥
+90 212 299 45 39
atamanmuseum.com

More than 60 gorgeous vintage cars from the 1920s to the 1970s are on display at this museum. After admiring a 1968 Alfa Romeo Spider or a 1965 Ford Mustang, grab a drink at the bar, which is befittingly inspired by classic American diners from the fifties.

5 places for great
LIVE MUSIC

416 **NARDIS JAZZ CLUB**
Bereketzade Mh.
Kuledibi Sk. 8
Beyoğlu ①
+90 212 244 63 27
nardisjazz.com

Istanbul's best venue for live jazz is hidden away in a backstreet by the Galata Tower. A cosy jazz club and bar on two floors, small candlelit tables face the stage where local and international musicians play the best of mainstream jazz as well as modern and fusion.

417 **SALON IKSV**
Evliya Çelebi Mh.
Sadi Konuralp Cd. 5
Beyoğlu ①
+90 212 334 07 00
saloniksv.com

An innovative and creative concert venue that can accommodate all kinds of performances due to a mobile stage system, Salon IKSV prefers the alternative and indie scenes rather than the mainstream. The venue's eclectic program includes everything from Turkish rap to classical piano to experimental theatre and dance.

418 **BABYLON BOMONTI**
Merkez Mh.
Birahane Sk. 1
Şişli ③
+90 212 334 01 90
babylon.com.tr

The first concert venue to have a professionally designed sound system when it opened in 1999, Babylon hosted such famous names as Jane Birkin, Charles Bradley, Patti Smith, Macy Gray and Lykke Li. After moving to its new venue in Bomontiada, Babylon continues to present the best of progressive music in its state-of-the-art live performance centre.

419 **BORUSAN MUSIC HOUSE**
Asmalı Mescit Mh.
İstiklal Cd. 160-A
Beyoğlu ①
+90 212 705 87 00
borusansanat.com

Located inside the headquarters of Borusan Sanat, the driving force behind the Borusan Istanbul Philharmonic Orchestra, the Borusan Music House was opened in 2010 to host concerts as well as contemporary art exhibitions. Shows are held only a few times a year but often focus on the very unique, contemporary and experimental.

420 **HAGIA IRENE CHURCH**
Cankurtaran Mh.
Topkapı Sarayı 1. Courtyard
Fatih ②
+90 212 512 04 80
topkapisarayi.gov.tr

The Eastern Roman Empire's second largest church, Aya Irini (Hagia Irene) is open to visitors as a museum, but with an architecture that fosters absolutely fantastic acoustics, the church is preferred for classical music concerts a few times a year, especially during the Istanbul International Music Festival.

HOTEL SPLENDID PALACE

25 PLACES TO SLEEP

5 *of the most* **UNIQUE** *accommodations*

421 **HOTEL SPLENDID PALACE**
Büyükada-nizam Mh.
Yirmiüç Nisan Cd. 39
Büyükada ⑧
+90 216 382 69 50
splendidhotel.net

Like something out of a Wes Anderson film, Hotel Splendid Palace harks back to Büyükada's more glamorous past with its art nouveau flair. From the all-white façade with bright crimson shutters and two silvery flagged domes, to an inner courtyard with vintage bamboo furniture and potted palms, every detail is absolutely splendid (including Café Spitz outside).

422 **ADAHAN**
Asmalı Mescit Mh.
General Yazgan
Sk. 14
Beyoğlu ①
+90 212 243 85 81
adahanistanbul.com

With a deep respect for the natural and pure, Adahan's rooms, inside an ecologically renovated 19th-century apartment building, are individually designed with custom wooden furniture and natural cotton curtains and linens. The terrace restaurant – with a beautiful view – serves homemade dishes from local and organic ingredients.

423 HOTEL EMPRESS ZOE

Cankurtaran Mh.
Akbıyık Cd. 10
Fatih ②
+90 212 518 25 04
emzoe.com

Rooms decorated with original Turkish textiles and folk art face the private verdant archaeological garden with the ruins of an ancient Turkish bath right next door. In the evenings the bar serves drinks in the garden (summer) or in front of the fireplace (winter).

424 THE STAY BOSPHORUS

Ortaköy Mh.
Ortaköy Salhanesi Sk. 1-A
Beşiktaş ④
+90 212 970 78 30
thestay.com.tr

Located right by the Bosphorus inside a beautiful historic mansion built by the Balyan family in the 19th century, the internationally renowned design firm Autoban renovated the building to become a modern boutique hotel. Enjoy the view and, if you can afford to stay in one of the penthouses, the private executive lounge.

425 SUMAHAN ON THE WATER

Çengelköy Mh.
Kuleli Cd. 43
Üsküdar ④
+90 216 422 80 00
sumahan.com

Once a factory that produced Turkey's national drink *rakı*, Sumahan was renovated impeccably to become a modern boutique hotel far away from the city. Lower floor rooms and the hotel's restaurant open up to a waterfront terrace, the private hamam offers relaxation and the hotel's private boat is available for swift transfers.

5 lovely
BOUTIQUE HOTELS

426 GALATA ANTIQUE HOTEL

Asmalı Mescit Mh.
Meşrutiyet Cd. 119
Beyoğlu ①
+90 212 245 59 44
galataantiquehotel.com

A beautiful neo-renaissance apartment building designed by Alexandre Vallaury in 1881 (for the French Levantine businessman Mr. Henri Hypollite Décugis and his family) is now the Galata Antique Hotel. Individually decorated rooms have a simple yet elegant design while breakfast is served on the roof terrace with a great Istanbul view.

427 GEORGES HOTEL

Müeyyedzade Mh.
Serdar-ı Ekrem Sk. 24
Beyoğlu ①
+90 212 244 24 23
georges.com

Inside a 19th-century apartment building with a very Parisian vibe in its muted elegance, Georges' rooms have marvellous views from floor-to-ceiling French windows, while the glass elevator leads guests up to the candlelit terrace restaurant and bar.

428 TOM TOM SUITES

Tomtom Mh.
Tomtom Kaptan Sk. 18
Beyoğlu ①
+90 212 292 49 49
tomtomsuites.com

Tom Tom Suites is housed in an elegantly renovated building originally constructed as the Soeurs Garde-Malades Apartment in 1901 for the Franciscan nuns. Stay in one of the twenty modern rooms and enjoy breakfast or dinner at the Michelin-star worthy Nicole Restaurant on the top floor with gorgeous views.

429 **CORINNE HOTEL**
Kuloğlu Mh.
Turnacıbaşı Cd. 41
Beyoğlu ①
+90 212 293 94 94
corinnehotel.com

Inside an Ottoman neoclassical apartment built in 1911 by the architect Kemaleddin Bey, the Corinne Hotel seamlessly brings together modern design with original antique touches. A great opportunity to stay in the historic Çukurcuma quarter, the hotel has its own art gallery and terrace restaurant.

430 **KARAKÖY ROOMS**
Kemankeş Cd.
Galata Şarap Iskelesi Sk. 10
Beyoğlu ①
+90 212 252 54 22
karakoyrooms.com

In another elegantly renovated 19th-century apartment building, right above Karaköy Lokantası (one of Istanbul's best restaurants), Karaköy Rooms offers retro-chic abodes that feel nothing like a hotel and more like a second home. Try to book one of the Deluxe Rooms with a marvellous sea view.

430 KARAKÖY ROOMS

5
REASONABLY PRICED
design hostels

431 **HUSH HOSTEL LOUNGE**
Rasimpaşa Mh.
İskele Sk. 46
Kadıköy ⑦
+90 216 450 43 63
hushhostels.com

A hostel that's soaked up all the genuine coolness of Kadıköy, Hush Hostel is decorated in street art murals and its rooms exude a comfortable simplicity. Cook your dinner in the communal kitchen, mingle with locals in the Hush Art Gallery, or just hang out in the lounge area, garden or roof terrace.

432 **BUNK HOSTEL**
İnönü Mh.
Papa Roncalli Sk. 34
Şişli ③
+90 212 343 00 95
bunkhostels.com

Inside the renovated Saadet Apartment, built in the early 1920s, Bunk Hostel is all about stylish accommodation that's affordable. Book a bunk bed in a room with other fellow travellers or opt for a private double room and enjoy a breakfast buffet on the terrace with a view.

433 **STAY INN TAKSIM HOSTEL**

Kamer Hatun Mh.
Balık Sk. 7
Beyoğlu ①
+90 212 244 88 08
stayinntaksim.com

Another hostel with a budget-friendly approach that doesn't skimp on style, Stay Inn is housed in a renovated historic apartment with a cool lounge and rooftop venue for breakfast and evening drinks. Try to book the double room with a terrace to enjoy a view of the bustling fish market below.

434 **HOSTEL BAHANE**

Caferağa Mh.
Kadife Sk. 27-5
Kadıköy ⑦
+90 530 933 56 35
hostel-bahane.business.site

A very cool hostel that's located in the midst of Kadıköy's most happening bar street, Hostel Bahane is for travellers who want to mingle with locals until the late hours. Clean and modern rooms, shared bathrooms and a lively bar and restaurant are all available to Bahane's guests.

435 **JULIET ROOMS & KITCHEN**

Caferağa Mh.
Şifa Sk. 31
Kadıköy ⑦
+90 216 348 70 00
julietistanbul.com

For a quieter stay in Kadıköy book a room at Juliet, a hostel on a peaceful residential street in Moda with its own outdoor cafe and a warm and homely décor. Shared rooms with bunk beds or more private twin or double rooms with their own bathrooms are available inclusive of a healthy Turkish breakfast.

The 5 trendiest

DESIGN HOTELS

436 **W ISTANBUL**
Akaretler Mh.
Suleyman Seba Cd. 22
Beşiktaş ③
+90 212 381 21 21
starwoodhotels.com

Inside one of the beautifully renovated Akaretler Row Houses (originally built for the Dolmabahçe Palace's workers in 1874 by Sarkis Balyan), the sleek W Hotel's suites have their own gardens, terraces or cabanas. Get a relaxing massage in the B&G spa, grab a drink at the W Lounge and explore the Beşiktaş neighbourhood.

437 MR. CAS HOTELS

437 MR. CAS HOTELS

Kuloğlu Mh.
İstiklal Cd. 153
Beyoğlu ①
+90 212 293 00 07
mrcashotels.com

Inside the graceful Güney Palas apartment built in 1884, this hotel really celebrates its historic art nouveau and art deco details. Thirty-three individually decorated rooms have custom-designed furniture in light colours that allow ornate fireplaces and crown mouldings to shine through.

438 WITT ISTANBUL HOTEL

Kılıç Ali Paşa Mh.
Defterdar Ykş. 26
Beyoğlu ①
+90 212 293 15 00
wittistanbul.com

Witt Istanbul Hotel is a discreet and contemporary boutique hotel that will make you feel like a cool local. Rooms are decked out in bespoke furniture by Autoban (the internationally renowned Istanbul design studio) and the roof has a permaculture garden and plenty of comfy seats to enjoy the amazing Istanbul view.

439 THE HOUSE HOTEL KARAKÖY

Arap Cami Mh.
Bankalar Cd. 5
Beyoğlu ①
+90 212 244 64 34
househotels.com

Inside a former Ottoman bank from the 19th century renovated by the award-winning architect Han Tümertekin, The House Hotel Karaköy makes full use of all its beautiful period details, including an original bank vault. Rooms in serene green and white hues have stencilled ceilings and beautiful green Carrara marble bathrooms.

440 GEZI HOTEL BOSPHORUS

Gümüşsuyu Mh.
Mete Cd. 34
Beyoğlu ①
+90 212 393 27 09
gezibosphorus.com

From its zinc and titanium façade to the wood and leather furnishings, the Gezi Hotel is all about contemporary design and a modern sense of comfort. All rooms, as well as the Fiamma restaurant and bar, look out over beautiful panoramic views.

5 extra **LUXURIOUS** *hotels*

441 **DIVAN ISTANBUL HOTEL**
Harbiye Mh.
Asker Ocağı Cd. 1
Şişli ③
+90 212 315 55 00
divan.com.tr

Open since the 1960s, the Divan Istanbul Hotel has managed to emanate sophistication throughout the different eras, especially after a thorough renovation process. Notable details include the modern lobby underneath a large sculpted chandelier of red glass, the Divan Patisserie with its heavenly chocolate eclairs and the elegant Brasserie with its menu of excellent Turkish and international dishes.

442 **ÇIRAĞAN PALACE KEMPINSKI HOTEL**
Yıldız Mh.
Çırağan Cd. 32
Beşiktaş ③
+90 212 326 46 46
kempinski.com

The former home of Sultan Abdülaziz is a sumptuous 19th-century palace by the Bosphorus designed by the famous Balyan family architects. A confluence of Venetian, baroque and Turkish styles, the palace-turned-hotel keeps the past alive with Ottoman-style décor and details, as well as a magnificent Bosphorus view.

443 FOUR SEASONS HOTEL AT THE BOSPHORUS

Yıldız Mh.
Çırağan Cd. 28
Beşiktaş ③
+90 212 381 40 00
fourseasons.com

The former Atik Paşa Yalısı, a stunning 19th-century Ottoman mansion, was restored and reopened as the Four Seasons Hotel in 2008. A bit more demure than the Çırağan Palace next door, the Four Seasons has a more contemporary décor in muted colours and a pool deck and bar steps away from the Bosphorus.

444 AJIA HOTEL

Kanlıca Mh.
Halide Edip Adıvar Cd. 27
Beykoz ⑥
+90 216 413 93 00
ajiahotel.com

Built for the Ottoman governor Ahmet Rasim Paşa in the late 19th century, this beautiful mansion was renovated and opened as the Ajia Hotel in 2005 with a contemporary interior design. Wake up to the sun glistening on the Bosphorus and enjoy your breakfast by the water.

445 THE ST. REGIS ISTANBUL

Harbiye Mh.
Mim Kemal Öke Cd. 35
Şişli ③
+90 212 368 00 00
starwoodhotels.com

Completed by Emre Arolat Architecture in 2015, the very modern St. Regis Hotel corresponds to the very upscale whims of the Nişantaşı quarter. In an art deco inspired interior of aluminium and copper, the hotel's luxurious details include a rooftop restaurant, a vast spa and butler service.

THE GLASS FURNACE

25 GREAT WEEKEND ACTIVITIES

5 of the best

SHORT WEEKEND TRIPS

446 **HINDIBA NATURE HOUSE**
Mengen Kıyaslar Köyü
Yedigöller Yolu
Bolu
+90 850 346 94 79
hindibadogaevi.com

Inside the spectacularly verdant Yedi Göller National Park, Hindiba is a real retreat amidst nature with simple wooden cabin rooms and plenty of walking paths through the wild flora and fauna. Produce from Hindiba's own garden and other ingredients from local and ecologically friendly producers are made into delectable homemade dishes, including vegan and vegetarian options.

447 **NARKÖY**
Kıncıllı Köyü, Yayla
Mevkii, Kerpe
Cd. 13-A
Kandıra-Kocaeli ⑨
+90 549 529 54 49
narkoy.com

A modern organic and sustainable farm and hotel with an educational focus, Narköy is the perfect place to learn about organic natural farming through activities and workshops. Dine on organic farm meals, stroll through the nearby forest and take part in outdoor classrooms.

448 CASA LAVANDA

Ulupelit Köyü
Seçkin Sk. 2
Şile ⑨
+90 216 736 56 40-41
casalavanda.com.tr

Certainly one of the most romantic weekend trips, Casa Lavanda is a family-run Provence-style boutique hotel in the Ulupelit village. Spend the day lounging by the pool, relaxing in the spa or hiking in the forest and enjoy exquisite dishes made by Chef Emre Şen from local ingredients in the hotel's fine dining restaurant.

449 BAKUCHA VINEYARD HOTEL

AT: ARCADIA VINEYARDS
Hamitabat Köyü
Lüleburgaz-Kırklareli
+90 288 473 44 17
bakucha.com

A family estate with an environmentally sensitive viticulture, Arcadia Vineyards also runs Bakucha, a chateau-style hotel among the sustainably cultivated vineyards. Guests can take guided wine tasting tours, join the seasonal harvest, relax in the spa and dine on local and seasonal dishes in the sustainable restaurant.

450 PARMA SOLE

Sahilköy Mh.
Kozalı Cd. 23
Şile ⑨
+90 850 333 12 12
parmasole.com.tr

Having lived and worked in Parma, Italy, the Yomralıoğlu family expanded their holiday home in Şile transforming it into an Italian destination restaurant and a boutique hotel. The menu of Parma local cuisine is prepared with ingredients from the restaurant's own farm and organic suppliers from all over Turkey.

5 very engaging

WORKSHOPS & CLASSES

451 **THE GLASS FURNACE**
Seniye İsmail Hanım Cd. 72-A
Öğümce-Beykoz ⑨
+90 216 433 36 93
glassfurnace.org

On the peaceful banks of the Riva River, The Glass Furnace (Turkey's largest and best-equipped centre for glass related arts) hosts fantastic daily workshops. From flame-working glass flora to sculpting animals in glass, hot printing on glass to kiln casting and enamel work, Cam Ocağı's deep passion and expertise is inspiring for novices and experts alike.

452 **COOKISTAN**
Dolapdere Cd.
Yunus Bey Sk. 32-A
Şişli ③
+90 535 574 50 10
cookistan.com

A cooking class (German/English) that specifically focusses on the uniquely multi-ethnic Kurtuluş area, Cookistan leads its guests through generations-old shops and the area's organic markets to shop for ingredients. At the Cookistan home, a six-course authentic Turkish feast is prepared and enjoyed with *rakı*.

453 LES ARTS TURCS

Alemdar Mh.
Incili Cavus Sk. 19, 3rd Fl.
Fatih ②
+90 212 527 68 59
lesartsturcs.com

Founded by a collection of artists, journalists and professional guides, Les Arts Turcs organises tours and workshops to allow travellers to get a hands-on experience of Istanbul culture. Activities include traditional Turkish felt, marbling, calligraphy, tile painting, henna and music workshops as well as tours to whirling dervish ceremonies.

454 NADAS ISTANBUL

Rasimpaşa Mh.
Uzun Hafız Sk. 80
Kadıköy ⑦
+90 532 166 76 15
nadasistanbul.com

Founded by Ahu Kopan and Jessica Sim in 2018, NADAS is a creative space inside a lovely 3-storey 1930s family home with a garden. NADAS hosts regular classes and workshops including a Tuesday art class and daily yoga classes as well as Green Square Meter, a plant shop/consultancy/hotel that hosts regular plant talks.

455 YOGAŞALA

Nişantaşı Mh.
Teşvikiye Cd., Celal Derviş Apt 16-7
Şişli ③
+90 212 241 00 67
yogasala.com

YogaŞala offers three free classes for all newcomers and has expert instructors in styles such as Vinyasa, Hatha, Ashtanga and Kundalini. A definite favourite is Yin Yoga in the evenings with Lebriz Dedeoğlu who rewards her students with tiger balm and herbal oil face and neck massages during final poses.

5 *great*

JOGGING ROUTES

456 **FROM KURUÇEŞME TO BEBEK**
Beşiktaş ④

The waterfront boardwalk on the Europe-side coast of the Bosphorus extends about 5 km from Kuruçeşme all the way to Rumeli Hisarı (with a few interruptions on the way). If you'd rather go for a shorter run, the route from Kuruçeşme to Bebek is around 3 km and can be rewarded with a delicious breakfast at Bebek Kahve.

457 **BY THE GOLDEN HORN**
Fatih ②

This is a shorter run that takes you across the Atatürk Bridge (make sure to enjoy a glorious view of the Golden Horn on both sides) and continues up the coast, toward Balat, on the boardwalk until reaching the small Fener ferry port and then back (about 6 km in total, there and back).

458 **THROUGH MAÇKA PARK**
Şişli ③

Maçka Park is not very big, stretching about 1 km from one end to the other, but can be a tad more arduous because of its hilly landscape. If you're looking for a longer route, you can run up and down the smaller paths that lead around the park's wooded areas.

459 BY THE MODA SEAFRONT

Kadıköy ⑦

Almost the entirety of the coast that surrounds the Moda area is a boardwalk where people love to run, stroll and ride their bikes. This particular run can go on for about 3 km in one direction and is accompanied by beautiful Bosphorus views the entire time.

460 BELGRAD FOREST

Bahçeköy Merkez Mh.
Sarıyer ⑥
+90 212 226 13 14

Once a village that housed the thousands of Serbs who were brought to Istanbul after the Ottoman Siege of Belgrade in 1521, the Belgrad Forest is now a verdant paradise of deciduous trees with hidden historic ruins. It also has a more than 6 km running and walking path through nature.

460 BELGRAD FOREST

The 5 nicest BEACHES *around Istanbul*

461 **MADAM MARTA BEACH**
Burgazada Mh.
Adalar ⑧

About a 20-minute walk from the ferry port (follow Gönüllü Caddesi and then Köknar Sokak), this beautiful cove is named after Madame Marta, one of Turkey's first ballerinas who lived on Burgaz island and was in love with the sea. Lovely in its seclusion, Madam Marta is also a great place to camp.

461 MADAM MARTA BEACH

462 **UZUNYA BEACH**
Demirciköy
Sarıyer ⑥
+90 212 204 07 33
uzunya.com

You'll only have to drive 1,5 hours outside of Istanbul's city centre to feel like you're on summer vacation. Located on the Black Sea coast, Uzunya is a great beach club where locals like to have their Turkish breakfast by the sea (even in the colder season), swim and lie around lazily in the sun.

463 **ELIO SEDEF BEACH**
Sedef Adası
Adalar ⑧
+90 216 382 48 84
eliosedef.com

Very similar to a cool Bodrum beach club, Elio is located on Istanbul's Sedef Island, which is only accessible by a morning and evening ferry from Büyükada or Elio's private boats (upon request). After spending the day swimming, grab some dinner and a sunset cocktail at the restaurant and bar.

464 **AKÇAKESE BEACH**
Ağva Şile Sahil Yolu,
Akçakese Köyü
Şile ⑨

About a two-hour drive from the city centre is Istanbul's seaside district of Şile and the beautiful beach of the Akçakese village. The turquoise sea and a white sand beach are quite popular among locals, so if you'd rather avoid the crowds, try to go here on a weekday.

465 **BAYKUŞ BEACH**
Gümüşdere Mh.
Sarı Çiçek Sk.
Sarıyer ⑥
+90 212 203 80 03
msgsusosyalislet meler.com

A very chill beach club run by the Mimar Sinan Fine Arts University, Baykuş (Owl) Beach is in the seaside resort of Kilyos about an hour away by car. Baykuş has plenty of sun loungers and umbrellas, a restaurant and a camping area.

5 hidden places only a SHORT FLIGHT & RIDE AWAY

466 MARDIN

After a one-hour plane ride and a short bus ride to the old town up on the hill, you'll become enthralled with Mardin's richly decorated stone houses from the Artuqid dynasty within beautiful labyrinthine streets. Make sure to take a daytrip to the equally mesmerising ancient town of Hasankeyf.

467 ŞIRINCE

Take a flight to Izmir (about an hour) and rent a car to reach Şirince, a beautiful isolated village where Müjde Tönbekici and her former husband restored a number of ruined historic Greek homes. Tönbekici now runs Nişanyan Hotel, an idyllic estate of renovated rustic cottages nestled deep in nature.

468 CUNDA

Cunda is the perfect little island covered in olive groves and historic Greek stone houses. Book a room at Otel Sobe (private beach available), buy olive oil from the local family-run company Kürşat and dine at their restaurant, Ayna. There's a regular bus service to Cunda from the Edremit airport (about an hour flight from Istanbul).

469 DATÇA

Fly to Bodrum and take a one-hour ferry ride to Datça, a seaside city and peninsula whose inhabitants have resisted large-scale touristic developments. Minibuses in the city centre can take you to all the highlights including Datça's old town, the ancient Greek city of Knidos and the natural coves and bays.

470 BEHRAMKALE

About a two-hour car ride from the Edremit airport, Behramkale is a small but immensely charming seaside town with historic stone houses set around a hamlet. However, the main attraction is the ancient city of Assos, where Aristotle himself once resided, and its Temple of Athena.

PRINCES' ISLANDS

30 RANDOM FACTS & URBAN DETAILS

5 *essential*
SURVIVAL TIPS

471 **ISTANBUL CARD**

The Istanbul Card, a refillable ticket card valid for all modes of Istanbul public transportation, can be purchased at the airport and at all newspaper kiosks around the city, costing about half of a one-use ticket. Refill machines are also available at almost every metro station.

472 **TAXIS**

Don't ever get into an Istanbul taxi that isn't connected to a taxi stand because you will get ripped off. Get into cabs that have some kind of taxi stand logo on their doors, or better yet, download the BiTaksi App to request reliable cabs with your smartphone.

473 **TRAFFIC**

Istanbul's traffic is like another concentric circle of torment and it can occur at any place and time so using public transportation is always preferred. If you have to drive/take a cab, check the very useful İBB CepTrafik App for a map overview of real time traffic congestion.

474 **PRINCES' ISLANDS TIPS**

Be aware that Istanbul's Islands, especially Büyükada, are uncomfortably overcrowded on the weekends. Animal rights groups are also still trying to have the popular horse drawn carriages banned because of the visibly malnourished and mistreated condition of the horses. You can show your support by avoiding the carriages and either walking or renting a bike on the islands.

475 **DRESS CODE**

Dress modest during the day when you're exploring the city, visiting mosques and historic neighbourhoods, walking through crowds and taking crowded modes of public transportation. However, you can dress as you like for hanging out at cafes, restaurants and bars in the trendier and more modern neighbourhoods.

472 **TAXIS**

5 *places to bask in*
ISTANBUL NOSTALGIA

476 VEFA BOZACISI

Mollahüsrev Mh.
Vefa Cd. 66
Fatih ②
+90 212 519 49 22
vefa.com.tr

Open since 1876 and run by the fourth generation of the same family, Vefa Bozacısı has remained virtually unaltered through the centuries. Order a glass of their speciality, *boza*, a thick drink made from fermented millet and topped with cinnamon and roasted chickpeas and admire the exhibited glass from which Atatürk himself once enjoyed his *boza*.

476 VEFA BOZACISI

477 VEDAT TEK HOUSE

Halaskargazi Mh.
Vali Konağı Cd. 41
Şişli ③

A remarkable visual medley of Ottoman and Western architectural styles, the former family home of architect Vedat Tek definitely stands out with its geometric cut-outs and turquoise tile patterns. Inside, you'll find the nostalgic Zihni Bar, which has preserved the original and stunning interior details.

478 RAHMI M. KOÇ MUSEUM

Piri Paşa Mh.
Hasköy Cd. 5
Hasköy ⑨
+90 212 369 66 00
rmk-museum.org.tr

There's nothing more nostalgic than admiring classic cars and motorcycles, locomotives, aircrafts and even a WWII submarine inside a former Byzantine anchor foundry and the 19th-century Hasköy dockyard. Of course a lunch break at the museum's elegant (and also very nostalgic) Café du Levant is definitely part of the journey.

479 ISTANBUL İŞ BANK MUSEUM

Hobyar Mh.
Bankacılar Sk. 2
Fatih ②
+90 212 511 13 31
muze.isbank.com.tr

Founded by Atatürk as the Republic of Turkey's first bank, the original İş Bank headquarter is now a museum rife with historic details. Inside the beautiful 19th-century palace-like structure, the bank's original teller stations and rooms exhibit the era's everyday banking objects.

480 MUSEUM OF INNOCENCE

Firuzağa Mh.
Dalgıç Çk. 2
Beyoğlu ①
+90 212 252 97 38
masumiyetmuzesi.org

Nobel Prize winning author Orhan Pamuk's Museum of Innocence might be based on his eponymous novel, but the museum also serves as a nostalgic glimpse into Istanbul's past. Marvel at everyday objects that paint a detailed picture of upper class Istanbul in the 1970s.

The 5 best Istanbul
MAGAZINES & WEBSITES

481 **CORNUCOPIA MAGAZINE**
cornucopia.net

An award-winning magazine that appeals to the more intellectual connoisseurs of Turkey, *Cornucopia* is an invaluable source of in-depth information regarding Istanbul (and Turkey in general). The magazine's website is also very useful including an Istanbul city guide and the best of monthly arts and culture events.

482 **THE GUIDE ISTANBUL**
theguideistanbul.com

Istanbul's first English language magazine is a visually curated and regularly updated collection of Istanbul's best venues and happenings in the food, shopping and culture scenes. Apart from the magazine (published every two months) and website, *TGI*'s Instagram divulges some great Istanbul tips.

483 **CULINARY BACKSTREETS**
culinary backstreets.com

Founded in 2009, *Culinary Backstreets* has grown to cover more than 12 cities (including Istanbul) and reports exclusively on traditional 'backstreet' restaurants that represent the city's true food culture. Their regularly updated website is full of great insider tips and *CB* also hosts culinary walks.

484 **MOMCIERGE**
hotelmomcierge.com

An invaluable website for anyone who is travelling to Istanbul with kids, *Momcierge* is a 'family travel concierge', founded by travel writer and mother Sevil Delin in 2013. Delin and her team provide babysitter services, rental equipment for kids, family tour guides and airport transfers with booster seats.

485 **212 MAGAZINE**
212-magazine.com

A bold and beautiful biannual magazine based out of Istanbul, *212* is reminiscent of other independent fashion and lifestyle magazines such as *i-D* or *The Gentlewoman*. Short fiction, interviews and long form reporting, as well as stunning photo essays, defy the usual and examine social, artistic and cultural phenomena.

5 *unique* NEIGHBOURHOOD NAMES *and their meanings*

486 KADIKÖY
Kadiköy

Continuously settled since prehistoric times, Kadıköy received its ancient name of 'Chalcedon' when it was settled by the Greeks in around 685 BC. After the Ottoman conquest, Chalcedon, which was a rural settlement at the time, was given to the first *kadı* (Ottoman judge) Hıdır Bey and was befittingly renamed, *Kadıköy* 'Village of the Judge'.

487 EMINÖNÜ
Fatih

A centre of trade during the Ottoman era Eminönü was full of sailors and traders going about their business as well as many *Emin* (custom houses). The neighbourhood's name was thus directly derived simply from its position, *Emin önü*, meaning 'in front of the custom house'.

488 ARNAVUTKÖY
Beşiktaş

Arnavutköy, which translates to 'Albanian village', received its name when Sultan Abdülmecid, who was keen on simplifying the lives of pedestrians, had men from Albania brought to Istanbul in the 19th century in order to work on paving the city's streets.

489 TARABYA
Sarıyer

During the Byzantine era, Tarabya became an area of healing due to its verdant nature and clean air and during the 5th century Patriarch Attikos befittingly renamed the neighbourhood Therapia (therapy in Greek). Over time, Therapia became Tarabya, a neighbourhood of historic architecture and excellent fish restaurants.

490 FERIKÖY
Şişli

A historic neighbourhood with lovely old churches and houses, Feriköy was settled by the *Rum* (Greek Ottomans of Orthodox Christian faith) during the Ottoman era. It's believed to have been named after the French merchant Monsieur Ferri who had his mansion built there in the 18th century. Over time, *Ferri'nin Köyü* (Ferri's Village) became Feriköy.

487 EMINÖNÜ

5 very enlightening **BOOKS** *about Istanbul*

491 MIDNIGHT AT THE PERA PALACE
By Charles King

A truly enlightening read that recounts a multitude of fascinating interwoven stories to detail the birth of modern Istanbul, author and professor Charles King deftly explores the interwar era. Tales of a tumultuous city without borders bustling with spies, artists, jazz musicians, exiles and poets allow for some understanding of Istanbul's enchanting essence.

492 A MIND AT PEACE
By Ahmet Hamdi Tanpınar

Often described as a 'Turkish Ulysses', Ahmet Hamdi Tanpınar's novel was originally published in 1949 and articulates the often conflicting facets that compose the Turkish identity. *A Mind at Peace* is a love story set against WWI and the cultural revolutions after the end of the Ottoman Empire and the beginning of the Turkish Republic.

493 ISTANBUL: THE IMPERIAL CITY

By John Freely

Written by the late and highly regarded American physicist, teacher and author John Freely, *Istanbul: The Imperial City* is a comprehensive study of Istanbul through all its various ages, from the earliest settlement to the present day, including an index of major monuments and museums.

494 ARA GÜLER'S ISTANBUL

By Ara Güler and Orhan Pamuk

Turkey's most eminent photographer, the late Ara Güler immortalised moments of daily life in an Istanbul that has changed so rapidly. This collection presents Güler's remarkable duotone photographs between 1940 and 1980 accompanied by the words of renowned Turkish author Orhan Pamuk.

495 ISTANBUL: MEMORIES AND THE CITY

By Orhan Pamuk

A deeply melancholic memoir by Orhan Pamuk filled with old black and white photographs, *Istanbul: Memories and the City* is a beautifully written account of a former empire trying to become a modern city, stuck between east and west and deeply intertwined with a young Pamuk's budding sense of self.

5 *amazing* ISTANBUL PRODUCTIONS

496 **ŞAHSIYET**
2018

A truly awesome Istanbul mini-series written by talented novelist Hakan Günday, *Şahsiyet* is about the aging judicial officer Agâh Beyoğlu (played by eminent actor Haluk Bilginer) who is diagnosed with Alzheimer's and thus decides to become a vigilante in a homemade cat costume punishing the perpetrators in an unresolved murder case.

497 **UZAK**
2002
By Nuri Bilge Ceylan

Uzak (Distant) revolves around the story of Yusuf who comes to Istanbul to look for a job whilst staying with his cousin Mahmut. Through Ceylan's iconic visual compositions that are more like paintings than film scenes, the loneliness and disconnect between two cousins is made palpable against a backdrop of Istanbul bedecked in snow.

498 CROSSING THE BRIDGE: THE SOUND OF ISTANBUL
2005
By Fatih Akın

A rollicking documentary about Istanbul's vibrant music scene, German musician Alexander Hacke meets (and sometimes jams with) the heavy hitters of Istanbul's rap, Anatolian rock, arabesque and indie scenes. Musicians include the psychedelic band BaBa ZuLa, Turkish rock band Duman, arabesque legend Orhan Gencebay and many more.

499 KEDI
2016
By Ceyda Torun

Director Ceyda Torun follows seven stray Istanbul felines in this fantastic documentary as they traverse the city and cosy up to their preferred human counterparts. *Kedi* is not only a glimpse into the lives of Istanbul's famous street cats, but also an intimate portrait of the city and its people.

500 HERŞEY ÇOK GÜZEL OLACAK / EVERYTHING'S GONNA BE GREAT
1998
By Ömer Vargı

One of those classic Istanbul films from the 1990s, when Altan (played by the now legendary comedian Cem Yılmaz) steals prescription drugs from the pharmacy of his brother Nuri (played by Mazhar Alanson, member of the famous band MFÖ), they end up escaping the Mafioso and finally bonding despite their clashing personalities.

INDEX

COLOPHON

EDITING *and* COMPOSING – Feride Yalav – ferideyalav.com
GRAPHIC DESIGN – Joke Gossé and Sarah Schrauwen
PHOTOGRAPHY – Elif Savari – elifsavarikizil.com
COVER IMAGE – Santralistanbul (secret 376)

The addresses in this book have been selected after thorough independent research by the author, in collaboration with Luster Publishing. The selection is solely based on personal evaluation of the business by the author. Nothing in this book was published in exchange for payment or benefits of any kind.

D/2019/12.005/5
ISBN 978 94 6058 2424
NUR 512, 510

Second edition, March 2020 – First reprint, March 2020
www.lusterweb.com – WWW.THE500HIDDENSECRETS.COM
info@lusterweb.com

Printed in Italy by Printer Trento.

MIX
Paper from responsible sources
FSC® C015829
FSC www.fsc.org